How to Fight Racism

Jemar Tisby has given us a gift in *How to Fight Racism: Courageous Christianity and the Journey toward Racial Justice.* I deeply appreciate the holistic approach to racial justice outlined in this book and am both challenged and inspired to apply the practical action steps that can promote racial equity. If we all step up and do our part, we can finally achieve racial justice. This book is an important part of moving closer to making this dream a reality.

CHRISTINE CAINE, founder, A21 and Propel Women

Those recently awakened or reawakened to the need to pursue racial justice who find themselves wondering "What's next?" will find the answer here. With authority, clarity, and compassion, Tisby invites readers of all races to join in a transformative journey of learning and doing, a journey marked by both resilience and hope. This is an invaluable book that points the way to deep and enduring change.

KRISTIN KOBES DU MEZ, professor of history,
Calvin University, author of *Jesus and John Wayne*

Jemar Tisby is a sociohistorical scholar par excellence! And he is committed to the advancement of the good news, for all. Tisby offers an unvarnished, biblical approach to antiracist work—one rooted in sound research, biblical knowledge, and a clear-eyed perspective on how white supremacy has made the good news bad news for so many. This is a critically important combination.

KORIE EDWARDS, associate professor of sociology,
Ohio State University

Jemar Tisby reshaped the conversation about race for white Christians with his bestselling, *The Color of Compromise*. Thousands of us came to see the way that our faith had been co-opted by the wicked ideology that sustains racism, and we then became desperate for concrete ideas to break the chains of this unholy alliance. In *How To Fight Racism*, Jemar responds to that very need. In this book, Jemar uses a very accessible framework of ARC (awareness, reconciliation, and commitment) to provide a road map for moving forward. You can be certain that you will walk away from this wonderful book feeling armed with a litany of practical tools for taking the next steps to confront and challenge this systemic and historic evil.

DANIEL HILL, pastor, author of
White Awake and *White Lies*

In this clear-eyed and practical book, Jemar Tisby brings his scholarship, faith, and humanity to the inescapable challenges of racial injustice in America. *How to fight Racism* is a timely gift and a biblical challenge. Read it, share it, teach it, live it!

CHARLES MARSH, Commonwealth Professor of
Religious Studies, University of Virginia,
author of *The Beloved Community*

With clarity and conviction, Jemar lays the path for anyone seeking to uproot racism in their lives, their families, their congregations, or any sphere of influence. Every leader needs this book!

NICOLE MASSIE MARTIN, DMin, assistant professor
of ministry and leadership development,
Gordon-Conwell Theological Seminary

The value of this book is that it is more than "how-to" instructions aimed at transforming society. This book is also an invitation to a journey of love. To some that will be disappointing; the author invites you to take that up with Jesus.

BILL PANNELL, professor emeritus of preaching,
Fuller Theological Seminary

This book is for people of faith who are ready to fight racism not merely by educating ourselves but by moving towards courageous action in diverse community. Jemar's work at the intersection of awareness, relationships, and commitment will serve the church as we seek to be reconciled, justice-oriented people. The varied narratives and concrete applications Jemar shares are in line with the integrity he has as a leader who is engaged in this multiethnic civil rights moment.

SANDRA MARIA VAN OPSTAL,
executive director of Chasing Justice

How to Fight Racism by Jemar Tisby has come at a perfect moment for the church. While racism in America is a highly complex, multilayered reality with a variety of definitions, lived experiences, and proposed solutions, the church of Jesus Christ stands as the only viable hope for ending racism. Even though the church has a mixed record when it comes to racism, it is our fight! If you're new to the fight or could benefit from a concrete road map to a more just and merciful society, this beautiful book makes the complex doable.

KAY WARREN, cofounder, Saddleback Church

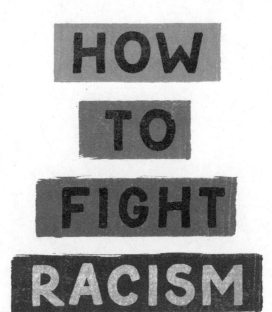

HOW TO FIGHT RACISM

Courageous Christianity and the Journey toward Racial Justice

JEMAR TISBY

ZONDERVAN
REFLECTIVE

ZONDERVAN REFLECTIVE

How to Fight Racism
Copyright © 2021 by Jemar Tisby

Requests for information sho0uld be addressed to:
Zondervan, *3900 Sparks Dr. SE, Grand Rapids, Michigan 49546*

Zondervan titles may be purchased in bulk for educational, business, fundraising, or sales promotional use. For information, please email SpecialMarkets@
Zondervan.com.

ISBN 978-0-310-10477-3 (hardcover)

ISBN 978-0-310-10515-2 (international trade paper edition)

ISBN 978-0-310-10478-0 (ebook)

ISBN 978-0-310-10514-5 (audio)

Cover design: Faceout Studio
Cover art: F. L. Wong / Shutterstock
Interior design: Kait Lamphere

Printed in the United States of America

20 21 22 23 24 25 26 27 28 29 /LSC/ 14 13 12 11 10 9 8 7 6 5 4 3 2 1

CONTENTS

Chapter 1

HOW TO FIGHT RACISM

Something is different this time."
I could hardly believe I had just typed those words in a tweet for thousands of people to read. I study history. I have the receipts of this nation's racial failures. I am a Black man in the United States.* I know firsthand that racism still pervades our society. I am neither naive nor optimistic about issues of race in this country.

But in the summer of 2020, a sustained movement of protests and uprisings began to roll through the United States and around the world. A viral cell phone video showed a white police officer kneeling for eight minutes and forty-six seconds on the neck of a prostrate Black man named George Floyd.[1] The officer killed Floyd, and once again a Black human being had become a hashtag. This person made in God's image and likeness became another victim of racism, anti-Black police brutality, and white supremacy.

Floyd's murder was just the latest in a string of similar

---

* Throughout this book, the word *Black* is capitalized when referring to the people group descended of people from Africa. This is because naming is a political act, a demonstration of power. For generations, Black people have been denied the power of naming themselves, of self-identifying according to their history, heritage, and personality. Capitalizing the *B* in *Black* is an act of reclamation and dignity. *Black* also refers to a racial and ethnic group, and capitalizing it coheres with other capitalization standards as in *Native American* or *Asian*. Finally, *Black* is the preferred term over *African American* because *Black* is inclusive of all people in the African diaspora regardless of their affiliation with the United States and connotes the global phenomenon of anti-Black racism.

events leading up to the 2020 protests. Breonna Taylor had been killed in a barrage of bullets in a "no-knock" raid by police who had entered the wrong house.[2] Video footage showing Ahmaud Arbery, a Black man out for a jog in a predominantly white neighborhood in Georgia, exposed three white men who pursued, shot, and killed him. They thought he looked suspicious because he had stopped to look in a house that was under construction. They became a law unto themselves and executed Arbery in what many characterized as a modern-day lynching.[3]

Christian Cooper, a Black man birdwatching in Central Park in New York, saw a white woman with an unleashed dog. The park regulations clearly state that dogs need to be on a leash. When he asked her to follow the rules, she called the police on him. Video footage showed her talking to the dispatcher and feigning an imminent threat from Cooper, who stood calmly filming her tirade.[4] Amid these and other similar events of racial profiling and anti-Black brutality, people once again raised the cry "Black lives matter!"

We had been through a round of racial crises recently. In 2014 and 2015, protesters had chanted "Black lives matter" in the wake of Mike Brown's death at the hands of a white police officer in Ferguson, Missouri. We saw the response of law enforcement, who came out with tanks, guns, body armor, and tear gas against people protesting for basic dignity and rights. Yet that wave of antiracist resistance rose and fell with little positive change.

We had seen the aftermath of a white supremacist entering the historic Emanuel AME Church in Charleston and murdering nine Black Christians after a Bible study.[5] We had witnessed the deadly "Unite the Right Rally" that brought together khaki-clad white people carrying tiki torches and demanding the protection of a Confederate monument.[6] We even saw the election of a president who regularly engaged in racist and violent rhetoric that seemed to embolden the basest desires of a certain segment of the population.[7]

We had no evidence that the results of protests in 2020 would be any different than all we had seen before. Yet I could not deny the facts. NASCAR banned confederate flags at their races. Companies such as Nike and Uber gave employees a paid day off to commemorate Juneteenth, the oldest celebration of Black emancipation in the United States.[8] The state flag of Mississippi came down. Confederate monuments came crashing down in cities around the country. Books about racial justice written by Black authors (including one of mine) packed the *New York Times* bestseller list like never before, as people clamored for resources to understand our racial moment.[9]

This time did feel different. The rapid shifts we saw could hardly have been predicted just a few months prior. But the COVID-19 pandemic and years of grassroots pressure for change had built up pressure that erupted in a flood of unexpected changes. I, as well as the countless others who dedicated their lives to the cause of racial justice, felt encouraged, exhausted, excited, and skeptical all at once.

Time will tell if the protests and uprisings of 2020 lead to lasting transformations in the United States. What is clear is that racial progress does not occur apart from the sustained efforts of people who dedicate themselves to fighting racism in all its forms. History demonstrates and hope requires the fundamental belief that when people of goodwill get together, they can find creative solutions to society's most pressing problems.

How to Fight Racism

I have been publicly speaking and writing about racial justice for over a decade. From the Pacific to the Atlantic, from college students to clergy members, the most frequent question I receive about fighting racism is "What do we do?"

A growing swell of people recognize the "fierce urgency of now" when it comes to fighting racism.[10] Maybe that's you.

You realize racism—a system of oppression based on race—is a problem nationwide and worldwide.[11] You understand that everyone is either fighting racism or supporting it, whether actively or passively. You want to be part of the solution. But you need guidance about what exactly you should be doing as an individual or within an institution to push back against the current racial caste system.

How to Fight Racism is one response to the how-to question of racial justice. While there has been a proliferation of books on race in the past several years, there remains room for more works that focus on the specific methods and actions that can promote racial equity.* This book prioritizes the practical.[12]

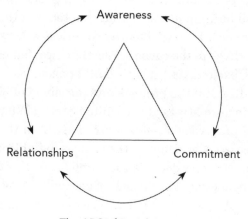

The ARC of Racial Justice

---

* Throughout this book I often use the term *equity* rather than *equality*. The Lakeshore Ethnic Diversity Alliance website explains the difference this way: "*Equality* aims to promote fairness. This is only effective if all participants have similar starting points and the same access to resources for achieving their desired goals. This approach can intentionally disregard the needs of individuals. *Equity* on the other hand demands that individual needs are taken into consideration. It accounts for identities (race, ethnicity, ability, nationality, gender, etc.) and circumstances that may otherwise hinder the success of one participant over another."

How to Fight Racism is structured around a model I created called the ARC of Racial Justice. ARC is an acronym that stands for awareness, relationships, and commitment. Racism uses an array of tactics to deceive, denigrate, and dehumanize others. As fighters for racial justice, we need to become familiar with racist strategies to effectively counter them. That's where awareness comes in. It is the knowledge, information, and data required to fight racism. Awareness is the "head" portion of the head-hands-heart triumvirate. In this book, you will discover ways to increase your awareness by studying history, exploring your personal narrative, and grasping what God says about the dignity of the human person.

All racial justice is relational. What sparks the desire for people to see change? How does someone develop a burden to combat racism? Often it comes through relationships with other people who are most adversely impacted by racist ideas and deeds. It is through knowing others that those we previously viewed as "problems" become people. It is by knowing other people, developing friendships and collegiality, that we can form the coalitions necessary to take on a society rife with racial bigotry. Think of relationships as the tender heart of racial justice. But often people stop there. "I have Black friends," they boast. We will address the shortcomings of such views later, but misapplications aside, you cannot pursue true racial justice without authentic relationships with people who are different from you.

Besides building awareness and developing relationships, what truly enables broadscale change on the racial justice front is a commitment to dismantle racist structures, laws, and policies. There is no amount of books you can read that will reduce the disproportionate rate at which people of color are incarcerated. There is no amount of probing coffeeshop conversations you can have that will shift the racial segregation present in our public schools. To enact society-wide change, people must commit to deconstructing laws that have a disparate impact on people of different races and rewrite the rules so they lead to greater equity among people of all races and ethnicities. Think of commitment as the "hands" aspect of the head-hands-heart metaphor.

The ARC of Racial Justice provides helpful shorthand for a comprehensive approach to race reforms. Many of us gravitate toward one area or one component of this fight. Some love to devour books, articles, and documentaries about race to increase their knowledge. Others do admirable work forging relationships with people from a wide spectrum of backgrounds and experiences. Still others are activists on the front lines of protests and leading campaigns for radical change. These are all admirable steps, but a holistic approach to racial justice includes all three aspects: awareness, relationships, and commitment.

Awareness, relationships, and commitment need not exist in *perfect* balance. The point of the model is not to practice an equal number of actions in each area. Rather, the goal is to keep all three areas in conversation and tension with one another. For instance, a college student can certainly build relationships and commit to racial justice, but college is an especially opportune time to build one's awareness through reading, writing, and learning from experts on campus. If one or two areas receive less attention due to your specific circumstances, that is fine. Just be sure to periodically assess where you are putting your energy and think about how your focus may need to shift from time to time. Keeping the three areas in tension and conversation ensures that no person or organization focuses on one area to the exclusion of the other areas. Rather, the three categories interact in a dance that changes cadence and rhythm according to the music of the moment.

The ARC of Racial Justice does not proceed in linear fashion. One does not progress from awareness, to relationships, to commitment—like following the steps to a recipe. Rather, you will grow in each area simultaneously, and sometimes one practice will build your capacity in multiple areas. For example, in the months leading up to an election, you may commit your time to helping potential voters get registered. During this season you may build your awareness of particular policies and platforms under debate in the election while also building new relationships with people in the community. The process of growing in awareness, relationships, and commitment never ends. You will always be learning, you will always be developing relationships, and you will always be discovering new ways to commit to a life of racial justice.

The Journey toward Racial Justice

The subtitle of this book is "Courageous Christianity and the Journey toward Racial Justice." Thinking of racial justice as a journey helps us focus on each step without growing discouraged when we don't make the progress we desire. The destination is racial equity and justice for people of every racial and ethnic background. The endpoint is harmony, where unity in the midst of diversity prevails. But viewing racial justice as a journey encourages us to think about fighting racism as an ongoing series of steps rather than a final point of completion. Instead of defining success by the results we achieve, we should define it by the actions we take. The effectiveness of our actions is not solely determined by their outcomes but also by the fact that we are taking steps forward and moving in the right direction.

As we begin to treat each other with more love and empathy, it will not only change the world around us; it will also change *us*. As I have taken steps to promote racial justice, I have developed more endurance, discovered untapped wells of creativity, and experienced more joy than I ever expected. The journey of racial justice is itself transformative.

On the journey toward racial justice, not all of us have the same starting point, nor are we all moving at the same speed. Black people and people of color have been fighting racism our whole lives. We have thought about racism, prayed about

it, cried about it, written about it, marched against it, and
resisted it as the very means of our survival. This is not new to
us. At the same time, we still have more to learn, and we can
always get better at pursuing justice. For some white people,
this may be a brand-new discussion. Perhaps you are just
starting the journey, and even baby steps are accompanied by
the risk of stumbling and falling. But you learn how to walk
one step at a time through persistent, informed practice.*

No matter how far along you are, thinking of racial justice
as a journey helps us move beyond the binary of racist and
not racist. In reality, everyone may act in ways that support
racism at times. People of color who have internalized racist
tropes may act in prejudiced ways toward white people or
toward other racial and ethnic minorities. White people may
support the racist status quo by choosing comfort and privilege
over the confrontation and change that racial justice always
requires. At times, even the most closed-minded person may
stumble into words or actions that promote equity. With the
humility of knowing that everyone's quest is different, our
challenge is to get on and stay on the journey of racial justice.

Courageous Christianity

While this book is intended for anyone who wants to work
toward racial justice, I have decided to approach this subject from a Christian perspective. I am convinced that
Christianity must be included in the fight against racism
for several reasons. First, Christians must fight racism as
a matter of responding to the past. Throughout the history

---

* Throughout the book I often use the phrase "Black people and other people
of color." Distinguishing between these groups highlights the unique experience of
Black people in the United States due to the existence of race-based chattel slavery. A similar distinction can be made for the particular histories of colonization
that Native Americans and other indigenous groups have faced. This delineation
does not imply that any group deserves more sympathy for the suffering they
endured, just that histories of oppression differ between people groups.

of the United States and colonialism worldwide, people who claimed Christianity as their religion have been the progenitors and perpetuators of racism. Theologian Willie James Jennings explained the concept this way: "Indeed, it is as though Christianity, wherever it went in the modern colonies, inverted its sense of hospitality. It claimed to be the host, the owner of the spaces it entered, and demanded native people enter its cultural logics, its ways of being in the world and its conceptualities."[13] As an illustration of Jennings' point, try this: Close your eyes and picture the face of Jesus. For many of us, we have to make a conscious effort to picture Jesus as a brown-skinned, carpenter from Nazareth instead of the European-looking image of Jesus with flowing auburn hair, thin lips, and blue eyes.[14] Visual representations of Jesus as European-looking are ways of making claims about religious belonging and authority. Christians wrote extensive and complicated works of theology to justify both race-based chattel slavery and racial segregation. When activists fought against slavery and racial apartheid, Christians were often the most vociferous and violent in defending the racial hierarchy they created and from which they benefited.[15] So Christianity must be part of the conversation about racial justice because, in the context of the United States, white Christians often have been the ones responsible for racial injustice.[16]

Second, Christianity provides a transcendent narrative for why racial justice is important. On one level, most people would agree in principle that treating other people fairly and not using race as an excuse for inequality are good practices. But why are these things good? What is it about human beings that means we should treat one another as equals? From whence do such ideas derive? As we will see in the next chapter, Christianity teaches that all people are made in the very image of God. We are God's crowning creation, and each person is precious simply because they are human. Their physical appearance—including skin color—are part of bearing God's image and should be respected as such.

Third, Christianity has within it the moral and spiritual resources to rebel against racism and white supremacy. Time and again, Christianity has provided courage for activists fighting for racial justice. One of the starkest examples occurred during the Civil Rights movement of the 1950s and 1960s in the United States. Theologian Soong-Chan Rah explains, "Civil rights is often seen in social and political terms. We often fail to recognize this movement as one of the most significant faith-based campaigns in American history."[17] Ida B. Wells, Prathia Hall, Rosa Parks, and many other foot soldiers of racial justice movements have counted on their Christian faith to give them courage to fight against racism.

Courageous Christianity contrasts with the complicit Christianity that led so many religious people to cooperate with bigotry instead of challenging it. In "Letter from Birmingham Jail," King wrote, "All too many [religious people] have been more cautious than courageous and have remained silent behind the anesthetizing security of stained-glass windows."[18] Courageous Christianity moves beyond the numbing safety of church walls and the comfortable Christianity that makes its home in segregated pews on Sunday mornings. It travels into capital buildings, city streets, farm fields, and wherever racial injustice may be found to demonstrate that the church is more than a place; the church is a people whose love for God compels them to act on behalf of their neighbors. Racial justice comes from the struggle of a small but committed group of people who choose courageously to stand against racism rather than compromise with it. Courageous Christianity dares to love through action and to risk everything for the sake of justice.

Setting Expectations

How to Fight Racism is an exercise in "prophetic imagination." In the Hebrew Bible, "The prophets voice a world other than the visible, palpable world that is in front of their hearers."

Filled with visions of a new reality, the prophets encouraged "an act of imagination by word and image that evokes and hosts a world other than the one readily available."[19] Oppression puts limits on our ability to envision alternate realities. By spending time exploring strategies for change, we may be inspired to create new ways to remedy issues of racism. This book is an invitation to dream. It is an open door for you to explore the possibilities of a world in which racism does not define so much of our reality, an opportunity to reimagine a life where we acknowledge our differences but do not use them to dismiss or dehumanize others.

People of any race or ethnicity will find helpful suggestions and ideas in the chapters that follow. The dynamics of race affect people across the spectrum of color, creed, and country. What is helpful for dismantling anti-Asian racism, for instance, will likely prove beneficial for fighting anti-Black racism as well. While most of the examples apply specifically to Black-white racial dynamics, broad applications can be made to the prejudice that other groups experience as well.

Many of the suggestions in *How to Fight Racism* pertain especially to white people because white people bear the most responsibility for racism. This has to do with a term that can be controversial: *white supremacy*. White supremacy is the belief or assumption that white people and their culture are inherently superior to other people and cultures. Or as Bryan Stevenson of the Equal Justice Initiative explains it, white supremacy is "the narrative of racial difference."[20] While I often use the term *racism*, *white supremacy* encompasses bigotry and racism of all kinds that gives social, cultural, and political advantages to those deemed white. If we want to fight racism, we must fight white supremacy as well. White supremacy is the reason that white people bear so much responsibility in the fight against racism.

To be clear, this book is not a how-to manual for forming multiethnic churches or increasing the racial diversity of communities of faith. Although some of the practices therein will produce greater diversity, I wrote *How to Fight Racism* to encourage people to go beyond the doors of the church and into society where so much of racism resides. The practical suggestions include things like political involvement, education reform, and expanding voting rights. The truth is that the racial segregation we see on Sunday is downstream from the racial segregation we tolerate Monday through Friday. As such, fighting racism has to be something that goes beyond a once-a-week service. It must become habit, practice, and disposition.

For those who have been deeply involved in racial justice, some of the ideas presented here will be familiar. Let us remember that potency in the fight against racism rests not solely on innovation but also on action. Even if a suggestion is familiar to you, now may be the time when you can finally put it into practice or when you can execute a strategy more effectively. Perhaps you will find new rationales for why you pursue certain methods. Maybe hearing them explained in a new way will spark new ideas. For those already engaged in the work of racial justice, the greatest benefit of reading this book may simply be the encouragement to keep going. You are not alone in this work. Your efforts are valuable and necessary. Reading about how to fight racism may refresh you on your lifelong journey in pursuit of justice.

Undoubtedly, some people who are beholden to the binaries of "left" and "right" or "liberal" and "conservative" will criticize the suggestions and practices I propose. Preexisting views about racial justice are shaped by political parties, religious affiliations, and polarized visions of the world as it should be. One of the major fault lines among people who hold different views of racial justice concerns whether racism is an individual or an institutional problem. Is racism mostly a matter of personal attitudes and actions, or is it the result of systemic structures and institutional policies? Those labeled "liberal" focus on the latter while those labeled "conservative" highlight the former. In this book, I am not seeking to pit the personal against the systemic. Individual agency matters significantly, even in a world where institutions wield enormous power. And institutional policies and practices can limit the personal choices and the number of good options that individuals have available to them. Racial justice must occur at both the individual and the institutional level.

Others may criticize the practices proposed here as "liberal," "leftist," "socialist," "Marxist," "Communist," or "promoting critical race theory." But such accusations are ahistorical. Some of these ideas for fighting racial justice have been offered for centuries. Extending voting rights to people of all races and ethnicities, for instance, has been around since the founding of the United States. Black activists and ministers have proposed the idea of reparations for slavery since before the end of the Civil War. Labels used pejoratively like those above typically ignore the continuity of racial justice movements throughout different historical eras. Instead of reflexively rejecting recommendations, test the ideas themselves for their impact on racial and ethnic minorities. Let mutual respect, humility, and solidarity with the oppressed lead you to your conclusions about what must be done to ensure racial justice.

Now for a word on structure: this book is divided into three main sections based on the ARC of Racial Justice: awareness, relationships, and commitment. Each section has three chapters, and each of those chapters contains an "Essential Understandings" section to outline necessary knowledge that will help you understand the "Racial Justice Practices" section that follows. In general, the first chapter of each main section pertains specifically to Christianity and speaks to the religious dimensions of racial justice that often get underplayed, overlooked, or misunderstood in the broader public discourse about race. These chapters will be particularly relevant to Christian leaders and laypeople who want to pursue racial justice, but they can be helpful for anyone who wants to understand more about fighting racism from a religious perspective.

I believe it will be most helpful to read this book in community. Processing the concepts will be more fruitful when you can hear other perspectives and experience the dynamism that comes from conversation with others who are on a similar journey. As you consider what actions you should take, start by choosing one or two specific actions from each chapter. You may want to scaffold the practices by choosing ones that seem easily achievable, others that feel like a stretch, and a few that may strike you as truly radical.

Above all, don't worry too much about where to begin. Just start somewhere. If you want a complete step-by-step plan for racial justice before you get involved, you will remain stuck in place. Often throughout history, people became activists because they took a single action. While there are always precursors leading to that action, there eventually comes a moment when a person decides that doing nothing is more costly than doing something. W. E. B. DuBois once said, "The cost of liberty is less than the price of repression."[21] When that becomes true for you, you will be ready to take the next step on the journey toward racial justice.

Sometimes people ask me what keeps me going on this journey. How do I avoid discouragement when racism seems to be winning the day? I certainly have seasons of struggle, doubt, and fatigue. But I find that remembering the ancestors in this fight fills me with inspiration and conviction to keep moving.

Fannie Lou Hamer has become an enduring example for me of what it means to practice courageous Christianity and move toward racial justice. Born as the youngest of twenty children to a family of sharecroppers, Hamer took up the family business of picking cotton at the age of six. Although she had a quick mind, she only attained a sixth-grade education in her formal schooling. White supremacy in the Jim Crow South dictated that tending the fields was more important for a Black woman than cultivating a life of the mind. After spending years as a sharecropper on a cotton plantation, Hamer might have lived and died in obscurity. But in 1962, at the age of 44, Hamer heard a civil rights presentation given at Williams Chapel Missionary Baptist Church in Ruleville, Mississippi, where she lived and worked. The presenters included James Bevel, James Forman, and Bob Moses, and they told those assembled about voting rights and how, by registering to vote, they could help elect officials who would work to uplift poor Black communities like hers. "I could just see myself voting people outa office that I know was wrong and didn't do nothin' to help the poor."[22] When they asked for volunteers to go down to the county courthouse to register, Hamer raised her hand as high as it could go.

While I cannot offer a full accounting of the momentous life of Fannie Lou Hamer, her story is worth knowing. She endured incredible hardships in her fight against racism. At one point white supremacists shot up the house where she was staying. White police officers brutally beat her and other Black activists in a rural Mississippi jail. Yet she went on to become a nationally known civil rights figure who, in 1964, gave live televised testimony of her struggles for voting rights at the Democratic National Convention. She also helped form the Mississippi Freedom Democratic Party as an alternative to the all-white southern Democratic machine operating in Mississippi at the time. She spent the remainder of her years working on behalf of the poor—both Black and white—in the Mississippi Delta.[23]

Hamer lived at the intersection of racism, sexism, and poverty. As a child of the Black church and with a mother who instilled in her belief in the Christian God, Hamer had a deep faith that empowered her activism and gave her indomitable courage in the face of life-threatening danger. In response to the threats she endured for her activism, she said, "Sometimes it seem like to tell the truth today is to run the risk of being killed. But if I fall, I'll fall five feet four inches forward in the fight for freedom. I'm not backing off."[24]

We need another generation of people willing to fight for freedom. We need a movement of people who will not back away in the face of racist evils and the lie of white supremacy. If you are willing to be part of this movement, and if you want to better equip yourself for the struggle, then read this book and take the next step on the journey toward racial justice.

PART 1

AWARENESS

Chapter 2

HOW TO EXPLAIN RACE AND THE IMAGE OF GOD

Kip Rhinelander was born in 1903 into a wealthy New York family. His marriage to a working class woman named Alice Jones in 1924 stirred significant controversy, and the two were considered a poor match because of class differences. He was wealthy; she was poor. But the economic disparities were not the reason Kip initiated a lawsuit against his wife in 1925, known as *Rhinelander v. Rhinelander*. When reporters heard about the interclass marriage, they set about investigating Alice's background and discovered that while her mother was white, her father was a biracial Black man. Some newspapers published the story. Under pressure from his father, Kip sued for an annulment of their marriage.

The case presented by Kip Rhinelander's lawyers alleged that Alice had deliberately hidden her racial identity from him in order to pursue a romantic relationship and marriage. "Before the marriage the defendant said she was white, not colored, and had no colored blood. She was colored and had colored blood," Kip's lawyer stated in opening remarks.[1] Jones objected that she had never hidden her identity. The bizarre court case lasted for a year. In a bold and demeaning gambit, Alice's lawyer offered his client's exposed skin as evidence of her honesty about her racial identity. Alice was required to strip down to her underwear and put on a long coat. She was then escorted into the judge's chambers, along with the all-white, all-male jury, where she was ordered to partially disrobe.

She was forced to show them her shoulders and legs up to the thigh in order to clearly establish her "dusky" skin color. The jury found in favor of Alice claiming that, given the intimacy of their physical encounters before marriage, there was no way Rhinelander could have missed her racially mixed heritage.[2]

Interracial marriage was legal in New York at the time, so the Rhinelanders had not broken any laws, at least none of those written in the books. They had transgressed the invented norms of a racial caste system that relied on subjective and malleable interpretations paraded as biological facts. What we now recognize as "race" is based on a set of customs and practices that are not immutable laws of nature. They are cultural and social inventions devised to create a caste system that keeps those imagined as "white" in a position superior to those categorized as Black or "colored."

In order to fight racism, we must begin with the fact that race is a socially constructed category that offers certain privileges and advantages to one group, which in the US context is white people, to the detriment of all those who are excluded from that group—that is, "nonwhite" people, or people of color.[3] Race intertwines with sex and class in a sticky web of exploitation and oppression. The concept of race has changed over time as often as society's norms have changed, and any progress in racial awareness largely has been due to the persistent protest of racially marginalized groups. But the ideology of race remains a potent force of oppression in the world today. This chapter expands our awareness of race from a Christian perspective and describes the foundational beliefs on which many of this book's racial justice practices are built.

Essential Understandings

Race Is a Social Construct

What we refer to as "race" is a social construct. This should not be taken to mean that race does not have real-world consequences. It simply means that race is a socially determined category rather than a spiritual or biological reality.

As we will see below, the Christian doctrine of the image of God teaches that all people have inherent worth and dignity simply because they are God's creation. This ontological significance means that no person of any racial or ethnic group should hold a superior place over anyone else because of their background or appearance. In addition to this theological grounding, science has shown us that what we call "race" is merely an indication of the amount of melanin in one's skin; 99.9 percent of our DNA is identical from one person to the next. Physicist, Riccardo Sabatini, explained that if we printed our entire genetic code on paper, it would take 262,000 pages and only about 500 of those pages would differ from person to person.[4] This minor biological variance does not set inherent limits on intelligence, cultural creativity, or social location. Instead, limits have been enacted by one group of people over another as individuals and communities made deliberate decisions to hold up one group over others.

The concept of race in the US context has three distinct features: it is elastic, based on physical features, and has social meaning. What does it mean to say the concept of race is elastic? Elastic means that racial groupings are not static or immutable. Definitions of who fits in to which racial category change over time. There was a time in US history when the Irish might not have been considered "white," yet over the course of decades they became firmly entrenched in the racial caste system as white people.[5] Those who were or were not considered Black oftentimes depended on skin tone and subjective opinion rather than ancestry.

In the United States, race has largely been defined in terms of physical appearance. It tends to be viewed as something related to hair texture, body type, and nose and lip shape. But skin color remains the essential feature of race. Anyone deemed nonwhite falls outside the highest level of the racial caste system; the darker skinned a person, the lower their position in society. People of color have even bought into the social construct of race. Among various people groups, "colorism"—a practice in which people of color discriminate among themselves based on skin color—remains a problematic issue. White supremacy, of which racism is a component, constructs concentric circles with white people of European descent in the center, the place of privilege and importance. Those in or near the center enjoy greater access to professional opportunities, more access to high-quality education, more financial wealth, and the presumption of innocence and normality. Outside of this central category are all other people of color including people of Latin American, Asian, and Native American descent. "Black" has been contrived as the "opposite" of white and, therefore, has always represented a marginalized status. No matter how much Black people attempt to assimilate by adjusting their patterns of speech, style of dress, and social networks, blackness in a white supremacist society can always be weaponized at any moment as a tool of dehumanization. This is why even when they were the President and First Lady of the United States, Barack and Michelle Obama, endured racist attacks.[6] No matter their level of achievement, people of African descent in the United States, especially those with darker skin, are always situated in the outermost ring of American social circles.

This is what a white-centered society looks like. This is why theology is simply called "theology" if it comes from European or white sources, but it is "Latin American" or "Black" theology when it comes from a minoritized racial or ethnic group. This is why for many decades the default color of Band-Aids was beige to match the skin of people of European descent. This is why Kodak, the camera and film company, calibrated all their colors to a photo of a white model, who was deemed "standard" or "normal," while people of other hues almost always came out under-or overexposed in developed film.[7]

Race has been created and re-created by social forces that change over time. No person of any race or ethnicity has a biological or spiritual claim to superiority over anyone else. Race has served to stratify society for the benefit of a few people who have been defined as white to the detriment of anyone considered nonwhite or "of color." Although race is something imagined (or constructed), its effects are real. From life span, to salary, to where you live, race has a tangible impact on one's quality of life.

How the Bible Talks about Race and Ethnicity

The Bible has something to say about race and racism. But looking to the Bible for explicit racial terms such as *Black* and *white* will likely leave you confused. The Bible, written over the course of centuries by dozens of different authors in various cultures and contexts, does not speak of race in the same terms as people in the United States in the twenty-first century. When Bible translations use the word *race*, they generally mean it in one of two ways. The first is in reference to the "human race," and this is usually to emphasize the unified origins of our common humanity. For instance, some Bibles translate the Hebrew word *adam* as "human race." "And he said to the human race, 'The fear of the Lord—that is wisdom, and to shun evil is understanding'" (Job 28:28).[8] In this context, *race* refers to all human beings without exception. Wisdom, defined in this passage as "the fear of the Lord," is something for the entire human race—no matter what their ethnicity or skin color might be.

English translations of the Bible also use the term *race* to indicate the difference between those who believe in Jesus Christ as the Messiah and those who do not. The first epistle of Peter reads, "But you are a chosen race, a royal priesthood, a holy nation, a people for his own possession, that you may proclaim the excellencies of him who called you out of darkness into his marvelous light" (2:9 ESV). In this instance, the term *race*, from the Greek word *genos*, does not refer to a person's skin color or other physical features. The word simply designates people who are part of God's new holy nation, the church, through faith in Jesus Christ.

Even though the Bible does not talk about race in the same way we commonly use it today, it still has plenty to say about how people should relate to one another across cultural and ethnic differences. It is important to remember that the individuals and groups discussed in the Bible came from diverse ethnic backgrounds. There are Egyptians, Israelites, Hittites, Cushites, and Jebusites, just to name a few. In the New Testament, when the Holy Spirit came upon the apostles at Pentecost those who were gathered spoke in languages representing more than a dozen different nations and people groups including Parthians, Medes, Elamites, Mesopotamians, and Cretans (Acts 2:9–11). So even though the Bible does not use our modern racial categories, it regularly records interactions between different people groups.

When the Bible describes the many different people groups of the ancient world, frequently it is speaking in terms of what we refer to as ethnicity rather than race. As J. Daniel Hays points out in his book *From Every People and Nation: A Biblical Theology of Race*, the term *ethnicity* is flexible enough to encompass language, nation of origin, and religion.[9] Ethnicity could include physical appearance, but physical features that may have distinguished one ethnic group from another were far from the only or even the most important differences.

A Brief Biblical Theology of Race

Throughout Scripture God reveals an unfolding plan for ethnic diversity that expands in scope from Genesis to Revelation. As we will see below, passages in Genesis 1 explain the doctrine of the image of God and provide the foundation for a belief in the basic equality of all peoples. Theologians call Genesis 3:15 the *protoevangelion*, or "first gospel," because God pronounces a curse on the serpent but promises deliverance for the people of God. He says, "I will put enmity between you and the woman, and between your offspring and hers; he will crush your head, and you will strike his heel." There is no indication in this passage that salvation will be permanently limited or differently applied to any particular ethnic group. Indeed, the passage implies that since Eve would become the "mother of all the living," the promise of salvation will be open to any of her children, people of all future ethnic groups (Gen. 3:20).

Further along, in Genesis 12, God expands the scope of the promised deliverance. When God speaks to Abram, God makes a promise: "I will make you into a great nation, and I will bless you; I will make your name great, and you will be a blessing. I will bless those who bless you, and whoever curses you I will curse; and all peoples on earth will be blessed through you" (Gen. 12:3). In these verses, God vows that through Abram's offspring he will bless all the families of the earth, an allusion to the international and interethnic frame of God's salvation.

Other passages in the Old Testament point to the global character of God's deliverance. Isaiah 2:2 says, "The mountain of the LORD's temple will be established as the highest of the mountains; it will be exalted above the hills, and all nations will stream to it." Again, it is clear that the good news is for all nations and not just one particular ethnic or racial group. Numerous other passages from the Old Testament suggest the same reality, including Isaiah 11:10–12; Psalms 67; 68; and 117; and many more. Throughout the Hebrew Scriptures, God's plan for salvation is built on the presumption of human equality and dignity and always assumes a multiethnic character.

In the gospel of Luke, we meet a man named Simeon who is waiting for the "consolation of Israel." When Mary and Joseph bring the baby Jesus to the temple, and Simeon sees Jesus and says, "My eyes have seen your salvation, which you have prepared in the sight of all nations: a light for revelation to the Gentiles, and the glory of your people Israel" (Luke 2:30–32). In the era in which Jesus was born, the religious and traditional divides between Jews and Gentiles could hardly have been more rigid. Yet Simeon recognizes Jesus as the Messiah whose deliverance would transcend the historical boundaries between nations and people groups.

Jesus himself, in his parting words to his disciples before his ascension into heaven, says to them, "You will receive power when the Holy Spirit comes on you; and you will be my witnesses in Jerusalem, and in all Judea and Samaria, and to the ends of the earth" (Acts 1:8). Jesus commands his followers to share the good news of liberation in ever-expanding circles extending from the Jewish capital to far away nations and people of every ethnicity. In Ephesians 3:6, the apostle Paul explains that the glorious mystery of Christ, a climactic unveiling of a truth hidden for ages but now revealed in the coming of the Son of God, is that "the Gentiles are heirs together with Israel, members together of one body, and sharers together in the promise in Christ Jesus" (v. 6). The good news of salvation in Christ was never intended simply for those who were ethnically or culturally Jewish. Rather, the promise of deliverance is for people of any race or ethnicity who would believe that Jesus is the Messiah. In this way, God forms a multiracial, multiethnic community of worshipers who will share in eternal communion with God and each other.

And in the last book of the Bible, Jesus offers his disciple John a glimpse of the goal of it all—the heavenly assembly: "After this I looked, and there before me was a great multitude that no one could count, from every nation, tribe, people and language, standing before the throne and before the Lamb. They were wearing white robes and were holding palm branches in their hands" (Rev. 7:9). The Christian picture of eternity is a multihued, multilingual, multinational, multiethnic fellowship with others in never-ending worship of the triune God.

From beginning to end, from Genesis to Revelation, God has planned for a racially and ethnically diverse church. This heterogeneity is not a mistake or a backup plan. Diversity is God's "plan A" for the church. In order to fight racism, people who advocate for racial justice must become aware of the scope of God's deliverance and the Lord's all-encompassing love for all peoples.

The Image of God and Race

Heavy rains drenched Memphis on February 1, 1968. But rain or shine, the garbage trucks had to roll. Two sanitation workers, Echol Cole and Robert Walker, took shelter in the back of an old garbage truck to wait out the worst of the downpour. But the truck was long overdue for repair or retirement. A wiring malfunction caused the hydraulic compressor in the back of the truck to engage. Cole and Walker could not get free of the truck in time. The compressor crushed them to death.[10]

In the wake of the disaster, Black sanitation workers went on strike. For years they had been petitioning the city's leaders for better working conditions, safer equipment, and higher pay. Now with the deaths of two of their comrades, a major movement began, one that eventually brought Martin Luther King Jr. to Memphis for what would be his last campaign. Throughout the strike, the sanitation workers used a simple phrase to communicate their core motivation: "I am a man."[11]

In various phases of the Black freedom struggle in the United States, activists have grounded their push for equal rights with assertions of their basic humanity. Phrases such as "I am a man" express Black people's insistence that they be treated as fully human—the same as white people. As the Black Power movement came to the fore in the late 1960s, the phrases "Black is beautiful" and "It is so beautiful to be black" adorned signs of protests and rallies.[12] Jesse Jackson helped popularize the phrase "I am somebody" by reciting a poem of the same name on *Sesame Street* in 1971. It soon became a catchphrase for civil rights activism.[13] And in July 2013, Alicia Garza, a Black activist and writer in Oakland, California, wrote a phrase on Facebook that would become a rallying cry for the modern Black freedom struggle—"Black people. I love you. I love us. Our lives matter." She wrote her post in response to the acquittal of George Zimmerman, the man who had killed Trayvon Martin (mentioned in chapter 1). Garza's fellow activists Patrice Cullors and Opal Tometi popularized the hashtag #BlackLivesMatter.[14] Black lives matter affirms the reality that the lives of people of African descent have just as much value as anyone else. All of these phrases evoke a sense of racial equality and are grounded in a claim to a shared human dignity and worth.

In theological terms, the phrases "I am a man," "Black is beautiful," and "Black lives matter" all express the biblical concept of the *image Dei*, or "image of God." In the first chapter of the first book of the Bible, God communicates the essential unity and equality of all people. Genesis 1:26–27 provides the basis for this doctrine:

> Then God said, "Let us make mankind in our image, in our likeness, so that they may rule over the fish in the sea and the birds in the sky, over the livestock and all the wild animals, and over all the creatures that move along the ground."

> So God created mankind in his own image,
> in the image of God he created them;
> male and female he created them.

Being made in the image and likeness of God means that human beings hold certain similarities with God. It means "that we all bear, in a limited way, characteristics of God's image: qualities such as morality, personality, rationality and spirituality that make us distinct from the rest of God's creation."[15] We can reason and think. We have emotions and compassion. We can make moral choices and have stewardship over the earth. Some of God's attributes such as God's omniscience and omnipotence do not extend to human beings, but God has crowned human beings with glory and honor (Ps. 8:5). As God's image-bearers, all people have innate dignity and worth.

God's fingerprints rest upon every single person without restriction. The image of God extends to Black and white people, men and women, rich and poor, incarcerated and free, queer and straight, documented and undocumented, nondisabled and disabled, powerful and oppressed. All people equally bear the likeness of God and thus possess incalculable and inviolable value.

Human beings do not simply *have* the image of God; we *are* the image of God, thoroughly and holistically.[16] Theologian Herman Bavinck described the image of God when he wrote: "This image extends to the whole person. . . . While all creatures display vestiges of God, only a human being is the image of God and is such totally, in soul and body, in all his faculties and powers, in all conditions and relations."[17] No part of ourselves is separate from our image-bearing.

If human beings are the image of God, then that image includes our skin color. The doctrine of the image of God teaches us that Black people and other people of color do not have to "become white" in any sense in order to be treated with respect. Too often in our society racial and ethnic minorities are forced to change important aspects of their identity in order to gain access to the opportunities others have. Whether it is one's pattern of speech, clothing, hair style, zip code, schooling, or interests, the subtle and sometimes overt message to people of color is, "In order for us to accept you, your color and your culture must go. You must become white." But the image of God teaches that no part of the way God created us has to be abandoned in order to gain the respect of other image bearers. God does not mistake unity for uniformity. God celebrates diversity.

In our Western culture, which tends to prize individuality, we can miss an important application of the image of God doctrine. Human beings do not simply bear God's image individually but collectively as well. Each people group with their various languages, dress, foods, clothing, and customs reveals a finite facet of God's infinite diversity. The kingdom of God is described as a banquet to which all, especially those on society's margins, are invited (Luke 14). Perhaps this banquet will be a potluck. Ethiopians will bring injera, Nigerians jollof, Jamaicans goat curry, and Koreans kimchee. Like a communal banquet that highlights the best aspects of different cultures, the heavenly congregation will put on display the magnificent diversity of God's people.

No single people group can adequately reflect the glory of God. Rather, we need the diversity present in the multiplicity of nations and tribes to paint a more complete portrait of God's splendor. But the sad reality is that the image of God has been denigrated in certain people groups. Historically, people of African descent have frequently been subjected to dehumanizing tropes and treatment by those who believe themselves to be superior.

Race-based chattel slavery stands as a conspicuous demonstration of dehumanization in US history, but the ending of slavery did not stop the dehumanizing treatment. In the Jim Crow era, white supremacists attempted to reassert their racial dominance after slavery had been abolished, with some using the Bible to argue that Black people occupied an inferior position by God's design. In 1900, the American Book and Bible House published a book by Charles Carroll entitled *"The Negro a Beast"; or, "In the Image of God?"* Carroll and those who agreed with him contended that white people descended from Adam and Eve but that "negroes" originally descended from animals. "If the White was created 'in the image of God,' then the Negro was made after some other model. And a glance at the Negro indicates the model; his very appearance suggests the ape."[18] Carroll held that Black people were simply animals that had the capability of speech and had been designed by God to serve the white man. So convinced of the soundness of Carroll's arguments were the publishers of the book that they declared if any of error could be found "then we are ready to close our doors, and place over its portals in burning letters of fire, 'Deluded and Misguided by an Array of Biblical Truths Scientifically Discussed.'"[19]

During this same period of US history, demeaning images of Black people gained traction in popular culture. The pickaninny, a patronizing epithet in itself, was a caricature of a

Black child. Artists depicted the pickaninny in disheveled clothes, unkempt hair, exaggerated facial features, and with a perpetually dim intellect. Similarly, the "mammy" character was a fictionalized Black woman dressed in the apron of a domestic servant, who always had a good-natured spirit about her relationship to the white family she served.

Today, seeing these images has become rarer, but racism remains institutionalized. White hoods and burning crosses are taboo, but instead we see poor Black and brown people shuffled into inner-city communities. Racism today comes in the form of mass incarceration and police brutality toward people of color. You can find it in the ongoing and widening racial wealth gap. It took a massive uprising for racial justice finally to compel brands to acknowledge and change their logos with origins in racial stereotypes, such as Quaker Oats' Aunt Jemima.[20] Native American activists and their allies have campaigned for years for sports teams to remove racist images and symbols used as mascots. Tropes of the "model minority" continue to be thrust on people of Asian descent. In every area of society—from politics, to economics, to pop culture—the denigration of the image of God in people of color continues. The fight is not over.

Affirming the image of God in people of all races and ethnicities requires sustained and intentional action. The section that follows gives several suggestions for how racial justice advocates can build awareness about the image of God and its importance in relation to race and ethnicity.

Racial Justice Practices

Teach What the Bible Says about Race and Ethnicity

Even though talk of racial justice has become more commonplace in many settings, one should not assume that Christians know what the Bible says about race and ethnicity. It is not uncommon for those who have the privilege of attending a seminary or graduate school in theology to encounter few discussions of race and ethnicity from a Christian perspective, and the ones that do occur may tend toward a superficial analysis that speaks in general of "equality" but has little to say about how believers should apply biblical teachings on racial justice to racist systems and policies. People in the pews also may have had little exposure to such teachings. So in the fight against racism, it is a good idea to start by teaching what the Bible has to say on the topic. Here are a few guidelines for doing so.

First, give plenty of lead-up time for whatever course of study you decide to use. Letting people know weeks or even months in advance that you will be talking about the tender subject of race gives them plenty of time to mentally and emotionally prepare. This will also give the presenters a heads up about potential resistance their constituents may have and allow them to build in commentary that anticipates those objections.

Second, remember to focus on community-building and trust. A small-group setting is often ideal for conversations about difficult subjects like race. For people of color, these configurations give space to be heard and develop relationships that may allow them to speak more freely and honestly. For white people, smaller groups may embolden them to ask honest questions that they would be afraid of asking in a larger group for fear of being deemed ignorant or insensitive.

If you intend to teach what the Bible says about race and ethnicity in a larger setting, then you can and should still spend time building trust. In a sermon, for example, statements such as the following may disarm listeners who already sit in a posture of defensiveness and skepticism:

> The Bible encourages us to "speak the truth in love" to one another. Some of us focus on speaking the truth, and we don't care who we offend. Others of us focus on love, and we avoid saying anything that might offend. The Bible

says neither of these is right. Instead, we learn from Jesus himself what it looks like to speak prophetic words of truth, no matter how much they may hurt to hear, and to do it all while loving other people so much that he would die for them. So today as you hear my words about race and ethnicity from a biblical perspective, please know that the goal is not to *unnecessarily* offend, but simply to speak the truth in love.

Finally, lay out what you've studied. The Bible talks extensively about national, regional, linguistic, cultural, and other differences between people groups. Once someone points it out, then it's impossible not to see the diverse world in which the Biblical text was written. Some learners will hear and immediately become gripped by a perspective on the sacred text they've never heard before. Others will have to sit with this information for months or even years for it to make sense. In any case, every Christian and any other interested party should have the opportunity to hear biblical insights on race and ethnicity from the pulpit and their church leaders.

Learn Theology from the Disinherited

Here's an exercise: Think of five theologians who have helped shape your thinking about religion. Write their names down. Now think of five theologians of color who have had a similar influence.[21]

If you have not been exposed to theologians of color, you may have struggled to come up with even one name. In many cases, we don't know about the significant body of work produced by Black thinkers and other people of color. There's even a chance we have been discouraged from learning about these theologies. But our understanding of the world and the Christian faith suffers from this lack of information.

In 1949, Black theologian and Christian mystic Howard Thurman wrote his most well-known book, *Jesus and the Disinherited*. In it he made a case for Christians to see how

Jesus identified with those the Bible calls "the least of these" (Matt. 25:40, 45). As Thurman put it, "The masses of [people] live with their backs constantly against the wall. They are the poor, the disinherited, the dispossessed."[22] While the world may overlook the people who have their backs against the wall, these are precisely the people who have the most to teach us about justice. Unfortunately, the disinherited of the world often have the least access to formal education, book publishing, and other platforms that would enable their voices to be heard loudly across the nations. To compound the problem, many theologically conservative churches and academic institutions rarely look to the theological resources of the disinherited as credible sources of knowledge. Instead, the books, sermons, and teachings of the disinherited are deemed theologically suspicious and referred to primarily as examples of what *not* to do in theology.

Any reformation in the way people think about race and ethnicity from a Christian perspective must include learning from people who have experienced marginalization and oppression. These include the voices of those who are sometimes called "liberation theologians." Black Liberation theologians such as James Cone and Albert Cleage Jr. along with Black womanist theologians such as Jacquelyn Grant and Delores Williams thought deeply about the implications of what it means to be Black in a white Christian environment. Cone wrote in his first book, *Black Theology and Black Power*, that Christianity was "in cultural bondage to white, Euro-American values."[23] His work helped to spur a movement of academic theologians who questioned this cultural bondage and proposed models of biblical interpretation from the perspective of the racially marginalized. Similarly, Latin American, African, Native American, and Asian theologies also provide helpful context from the perspective of the poor and the politically oppressed as they looked to their faith to both explain and change their circumstances.

Unfortunately, some people have been so conditioned to distrust nonwhite or non-European theological sources that they will not even consider the possibility of learning from them. They believe "liberation theology" derives from a fundamental misreading of Scripture and is heresy. You may have to contend with these objections as you seek to glean wisdom from nonwhite sources in any field, whether theology or history or science. It should be self-evident, but people often need to be reminded that listening to others and even coming to appreciate one idea or part of a system of thought, philosophy, or theology does not necessarily mean you are endorsing every aspect of that system.

We all tend to selectively critique theological systems based on our cultural preferences and assumptions. Theologies developed by people of color should not receive any more or less scrutiny than those devised by European and white people. I believe there is much to learn from the theological insights of Palestinians, indigenous peoples, and Latin Americans, just to name a few. Yet I find it odd that some people seem more willing to learn from the theologies of slaveholders than the theologies of the enslaved and oppressed. The presumed theological and intellectual superiority of European and white sources is itself an example of white supremacy and should be confronted whenever you teach about biblical ideas of race and ethnicity.

Treat Racism as It Should Be Treated: Like a Sin

Here was an announcement you almost never see: "The [Executive Committee] has voted, on behalf of the SBC, to withdraw fellowship from Raleigh White Baptist Church in Albany, Ga., based on 'clear evidence' of racial discrimination."[24] In 2018, the Southern Baptist Convention had voted to officially expel a member church for racism.

Raleigh White Baptist Church, named after a former pastor, had seen its membership dwindle from more than 200 down to 20 people. The church, located in the majority Black town of Albany, Georgia, had agreed to share its building with a Black church called New Seasons in what they hoped would be a mutually beneficial arrangement. But the relationship quickly soured and the members of Raleigh White gave a cold shoulder to the members of New Seasons. Despite working with a mediator, the white churchgoers never warmed to the Black members of New Seasons.

One Sunday in March, Raleigh White Baptist church planned a "homecoming" service for its former members, and they advised New Seasons that it would have to change the time of their service to a later hour to accommodate the occasion. The members of New Seasons agreed, but when some Black churchgoers came early to set up for their service, they were turned away. "If you were white, you could go into the church. If you were black, you were not allowed in," the pastor of New Seasons, Marcus Glass, said.[25]

In response, the local Baptist association expelled Raleigh White Baptist Church. Then the Southern Baptist Convention followed suit based on "clear evidence" of racial discrimination. As Hans Wunch, a spokesperson for the Mallary Baptist Convention said, "We wanted to think this was something besides racism. But it just became overly clear that it became a component to what was going on. . . . We could not associate with that anymore."[26]

What happened to Raleigh White Baptist Church almost never happens—clear, disciplinary action in response to racism. While few churches would argue against the idea that racism is a sin, most will not deal with it as such. Too often racism is treated like an unlikable personality trait—something unsavory but not sinful. Yet if white Christians treated racism as the sin that it is, more people and churches would have to come under church discipline for their racist beliefs and actions. Instead, people and organizations that act in racist ways can continue as members in good standing at many Christian churches and denominations.

To truly raise awareness about the threat of racism, white Christians should be prepared to bring formal charges against those who practice racism in word or deed. I am aware this presents certain challenges. People may not know they are being racist, or they may not intend to be so. It is also difficult to "prove" that a person or group meant to be racist. There may not be "hard" evidence of such intentions, even if the result is clearly racist. And if a person demonstrates humility and contrition once their offense is revealed, they should be allowed the opportunity to repent and walk through a process of repair. All too often, however, people proudly cling to their bigotry. They insist they are right and refuse to change their stance. In these cases, I suggest following the disciplinary procedure outlined in Matthew 18 and in many denominational standards. Matthew 18:15–20 instructs Christians who have been sinned against to address the offender one-on-one (if it is safe to do so). If they change their ways after that, then the matter is done. But if they refuse to admit their fault, then the offended party should come back and lovingly confront the person with an additional witness or two. If they still refuse to listen, then the matter is to be taken to the entire congregation. If the offender continues in their obstinance, then they are to be treated like a "pagan" or a "tax collector"—someone hostile to the faith or to the community.

Yet how often was this procedure followed to address racism in the Christian church? In the Jim Crow era, how many Christians showed up to a lynching on Saturday and then went to church on Sunday? How many acted as jurors in clear cases when a Black person's civil rights were violated but still voted to acquit in the 1950s and 1960s? How many swindled people of color in their business dealings and used their filthy lucre to donate to the church? In order to fight for racial justice, racism must not be lightly dismissed. It must be treated as the evil offense against God and human beings that it is.

The suggestions given above are just a few of the ways that churches can educate their congregations about race and ethnicity from a biblical perspective. Much more remains to be said about the specific actions that churches can take to promote racial justice, and I will address that in later chapters.

But we should never assume that just because someone says they are a Christian, they know what the Bible teaches about race, ethnicity, and equality. Building awareness means explaining and applying the biblical teaching of the image of God and what that means for racial justice today.

Chapter 3

HOW TO EXPLORE YOUR RACIAL IDENTITY

She spoke with a tone of bewilderment in her voice—as if she was still absorbing events that had happened years ago—yet she spoke confidently, freely sharing the details of her story. Teboho, a young Black South African woman, was sharing her testimony before members and guests at a new church in Cape Town. She spoke about the #FeesMustFall movement of 2015, when she saw how white Christians responded with obstinacy and criticism instead of compassion and understanding.[1]

In 2015, officials at the University of Witwatersrand in Johannesburg announced a fee (tuition) increase of 10.5 percent for the upcoming school year.[2] In response, Black South Africans led the way in protesting an increase in school fees that would have locked out many Black people from a quality education that they could not afford. They used the phrase "fees must fall" as a mobilizing phrase for the movement. As the movement gained momentum, Christians from across the color line weighed in. Some Christian groups initially came out in support of the protestors, but other Christians saw #FeesMustFall as confrontational, divisive, and violent. They launched the #colourblind initiative as a way to advocate for "unity, reconciliation and a stop to racism 'from all races.'"[3]

"For the first time I realized that my brothers and sisters in Christ when it came to this issue we are not on the same page. I was so confused. I still did not have the vocabulary for it," Teboho explained.[4] Teboho had become a Christian through the ministry of a predominantly white church, and these people were her spiritual family, her trusted friends, her brothers and sisters in the household of faith. Yet when it came to matters that affected her daily life as a Black person, this group of people felt like strangers to her. Teboho shared that she often experienced greater commonality with people who did not share her religion. "It was interesting that you could relate more to those who do not confess the faith than those who did. Even the white people who were not Christian somewhat 'got it.' [They understood] the injustice in access to education."[5] Black Christians and other oppressed people often find solidarity with those working for justice, even if they do not share the same spiritual convictions. Teboho's realization during the #FeesMustFall movement initiated a process of spiritual reevaluation for her. "So for me at this stage it's a healing process and a lamenting and repenting. . . . And also realizing [that] how the Bible is taught to us is important."[6]

A pressing issue of racial justice forced Teboho to reconsider what it meant to be both Black and Christian. She had been taught by white Christians that the gospel of Jesus Christ is the great unifier. But when the reality of racism demanded a response, she found there were limits to white Christian support. Despite this sense of betrayal by white Christians, she did not lose her faith. She embraced her Blackness as part of what it means to be fully human.

Essential Understandings

Racial Identity Development

Teboho's story is all too common. Many Black Christians in the United States have shared similar experiences during the height of the #BlackLivesMatter movement. Throughout history people of color have had to endure racial awakenings that destabilized their foundational beliefs about faith, society, self, and others.

Just as Teboho initially lacked the words to describe this experience, people can often struggle to name what they are going through as they develop a greater sense of racial awareness. But social scientists have a name for what it means to discover a sense of one's race. It's called racial identity development, and this chapter explains the crucial need for people of all races to critically explore their racial identity and ensure they are moving in a direction toward greater self-awareness and sensitivity.

One of the most thorough contemporary treatments of racial identity development comes from Dr. Beverly Daniel Tatum, a social psychologist and the former president of Spelman College in Atlanta. In 1997, she wrote a book called *Why Are All the Black Kids Sitting Together in the Cafeteria, and Other Conversations about Race*, and the book proved to be so helpful she wrote a revised and updated edition in 2017. In it, Tatum defines "racial identity" as "the meaning each of us has constructed or is constructing about what it means to be a White person or a person of color in a race-conscious society."[7] Notice that racial identity is not just for Black people and other people of color. White people have a racial identity that must be explored as well. Similarly, "racial identity development" refers to "the process of defining for oneself the personal significance and social meaning of belonging to a particular racial group."

William Cross developed the model for racial identity development for Black people in 1971.[8] Since Cross first developed his model, other psychologists have created models for other people groups, including biracial, immigrants, and white people. In general, the stages of identity development move from unawareness, typically at younger ages, to greater awareness as people get older and have more interactions with others. The tables below, adapted from Cross's original model, detail the stages of racial identity development. People of color are represented by the first model, and white people by the second.[9]

Racial/Cultural Identity Development Model[10]

Stages of Minority Development Model	Attitude toward Self	Attitude toward Others of the Same Minority	Attitude toward Others of a Different Minority	Attitude toward Dominant Group
Stage 1: Conformity	Has absorbed the images, beliefs, values of dominant group. Considers self as "colorblind" and the world as "raceless." Views the world individualistically and relationally; unaware of significance of group.	Identifies with and seeks acceptance among the dominant group, often by downplaying aspects associated with the dominant group.	Disinterest; distance. Co-ethnics may reject him/her because of assimilation to the dominant group.	"Don't call me ___; I'm American." "We're all just people." "Just treat me as the individual I am." "___ are so uncool." "Why do they only stick to themselves?"
Stage 2: Dissonance and appreciating	If positive encounter, surprised by perceived differences. If negative encounter, feels devalued and rejected; now unsure of own identity and community. Earlier beliefs about equality, "liberty and justice for all" shaken.	Hurt, anger, confusion. May develop an "oppositional" identity, both protecting self and keeping the dominant group at a distance. Invalidating responses result in further disengagement.	Openness to reconsidering the significance of ethnicity.	"My color wasn't supposed to matter, but clearly it does matter to them after all." "She's different—how could she be proud of being Black?"

Stages of Minority Development Model	Attitude toward Self	Attitude toward Others of the Same Minority	Attitude toward Others of a Different Minority	Attitude toward Dominant Group
Stage 3: Resistance and immersion	Redefining self.	Little interest in developing relationships outside the group; outsiders are irrelevant.	Joins peer group, which becomes the new social network. Seeks positive images and history; surrounds self with symbols of identity.	"Black is beautiful." "Whites are so uptight."
Stage 4: Introspection	The new identity is integrated into the self-concept and affirmed; a new sense of security results.	Willing to establish meaningful relationships across group boundaries with those who respect the new self-definition.	The ethnic identity and ethnic social network are consciously embraced.	"Say it strong and say it loud: I'm Black and I'm proud!"
Stage 5: Integrative Awareness	"Emissary": sees own achievement as advancing the group's cause.	Prepared to cross and transcend group boundaries as an emissary.	Willing to act as spokesperson and advocate for the group. Prepared to function more effectively in diverse settings.	"I can learn from both Latinos and Whites."

Source: William Cross, *Shades of Black: Diversity in African American Identity*, cited in Beverly Daniel Tatum, *Why Are All the Black Kids Sitting Together in the Cafeteria?* (New York: Basic, 1997), adapted and elaborated by Lisa Sung** (2/2002).[11]

Stages of Racial Identity Development: White Identity

Stage	Self-Perception	Stance toward Own (Dominant) Group	Stance toward People of Color	Typical Perceptions & Perceptions
1. Pre-Contact Whites pay little attention to the significance of their racial identity "I am normal." "I'm colorblind."	"Normal": no particular culture or ethnicity. Sees self as a person of goodwill, unprejudiced, colorblind. Views persons and the world individualistically and relationally; unaware of significance of group.	"Normal." Sees own community as possessing goodwill, unprejudiced, colorblind. Racism is deliberate and over: acts of hostility or discrimination, or hate crimes committed by certain individuals.	Disinterest or naïve curiosity about ethnic or cultural differences.	"I don't see color. I treat all the kids the same." "I don't see why they keep focusing on our differences; underneath, we're all the same." "Why do those Hispanics always stick to each other?" "I don't think of you as ___; you're just you." "Some of my best friends are ___."
2. Disintegration Growing awareness of racism and white privilege as a result of personal encounters. This new awareness is characterized by discomfort. "How can I be white?"	Earlier beliefs about equality, "liberty and justice for all" shaken. Feelings of guilt and shame about historical oppression and about one's own status in light of White privilege.	Anger. Tempted to distance self from confronting the issues and one's upbringing and community. May retreat into silence, or may become overzealous.	Sees impact of racism in life of associate or friend. May react by trying to dissociate completely from own group and to become "adopted" by people of color.	"I'm not like most Whites; I'm a very fair, compassionate person." "I can't stand his racist jokes any longer." "I am a religious and moral person, but how do I accept this injustice?"

Stage	Self-Perception	Stance toward Own (Dominant) Group	Stance toward People of Color	Typical Perceptions & Perceptions
3. Reintegration Idealization of Whites and White culture and denigration of people of color and their cultures. "We have the best because we are the best."	Denial of responsibility for the problems of people of color. Blaming the victim and reasserting the cultural myths of rugged individualism and of pure meritocracy.	Sides with and justifies the actions of own group and the pursuit of group interest.	Hostility and anger directed toward people of color. Negative stereotypes and fear of people of color.	"I'm not responsible for society or the hate of a few." "Everybody can succeed if they just work hard, so they have only themselves to blame." "I don't know why these parents keep playing the race card."
4. Pseudo-Independent The individual gains an *intellectual* understanding of racism as a system of advantage, but unsure what to do about it. "Let's help them become more like Whites."	May develop "aversive racism": wants the ideals of equality and racial tolerance, yet unwilling to confront own racialized biases and racialized privilege.	Tends to overlook and rationalize racializing biases and actions perpetuating White privilege, by 1) denying that prejudice exists, or 2) citing other reasons.	May try escaping Whiteness by exclusively associating with people of color; maybe rebuffed by those in the Dissonance or Resistance/ immersion stages. Localizes race and race issues in people of color.	"Achievement gap has nothing to do with race; it's all about poverty." "Let's teach Hispanic parents how to be better parents at home." "He didn't mean to be racist. He's a nicest guy I've ever known." "What does research say?"

(cont.)

Stage	Self-Perception	Stance toward Own (Dominant) Group	Stance toward People of Color	Typical Perceptions & Perceptions
5. Immersion Marked by a recognized need to find more positive self-definition. Whites need to seek new ways of thinking about Whiteness, ways that take them behind the role of victimizer. "I'm white!"	Wants to develop a positive self-concept as a White in light of the historical and contemporary reality of White privilege. Assumes personal responsibility for racism and understand one's role in perpetuating it.	Wants to develop a positive self-concept as a White in light of the historical and contemporary reality of White privilege.	If successful in forming relationships with people of color, may benefit from their outside perspective and comparison.	"I don't know anything about my ethnicity or culture; I feel a little cheated. Whey didn't my family keep alive?" "If I really start speaking up about racism, I might start losing friends over it. Do I really want to get into with it them?"
6. Integration A person incorporates the newly defined view of whiteness as part of a personal identity. The process is marked by an increased effectiveness in multiracial settings. Continued engagement in learning about anti-racism. "I see color and I like it."	Positive views of European American ethnic identity and of whiteness are internalized. Makes a commitment to oppose racism.	Committed to act and advocate for justice for people of color by seeking to dismantle White privilege and by working for full inclusion.	Committed to act to advocate for justice and to work to empower people of color for full participation and contribution.	"What can I do to help all people see the impact of race in student learning?" "How can I work with my allies to reduce racial disparities in student discipline?"

Source: Janet Helms (1990).

One of the most valuable aspects of learning the racial-ethnic-cultural identity model is that it gives a framework for different stages of racial awareness. The word *development* indicates a process of change—racial identity is not static. If you can locate which stage of racial-ethnic-cultural identity you are at presently, then you can more intentionally move toward racial maturity and awareness.

Racial Justice Practices

Locate Where You Are in Your Racial/ Cultural Identity Development

The different phases of racial identity development include: conformity, dissonance, resistance and immersion, introspection, and integrative awareness. In general, one begins with less awareness of racial dynamics and an unconscious acceptance of white people and their cultural practices as normative, acceptable, and even preferred. Teboho, the Black South African woman at the beginning of the chapter, might have been moving from conformity to dissonance in her racial identity development. The #FeesMustFall movement helped her realize that racial solidarity with other Black South Africans meant conflict with her white Christian community. If she'd had this model to guide her thinking, Teboho might have more easily found the language she needed to express her racial journey. Knowing where you are in your own racial identity development can help you name the emotions you are feeling and can move you toward more mature levels of racial awareness.

At some point in life, most people have an encounter with racism that disrupts their previous thinking. In the United States, some Native Americans may have been catalyzed by the protests against the construction of the Dakota Access Pipeline (#NoDAPL). People of Latin American descent have rallied to oppose family separation at the border between the

United States and Mexico. For young Black people, the murders of George Floyd and Breonna Taylor have been catalysts for racial awareness and activism. These disruptive events sometimes jolt Black people and other people of color into a new recognition of the salience of race in their own lives and the broader culture. The "dissonance and appreciation" phase of racial identity development requires a reassessment of your previous racial paradigms and begins a process of exploring your own racial or ethnic group with more intentionality.

In a white-centered society, white people have their own process of racial identity development. White people tend to grow up with a "colorblind" mentality, meaning they are taught to not "see color," and that the only way to treat everyone equally is to pretend that everyone is the same. In the bestselling book *White Fragility*, Robin DiAngelo lists several statements that may indicate a person has accepted the theory of colorblindness.

"I was taught to treat everyone the same."
"I don't care if you're pink, purple, or polka-dotted."
"Focusing on race is what divides us."[12]

Yet the theory of colorblindness denies the historic and tangible ways that race affects people of color and shapes the thinking and behaviors of white people. The lens of colorblindness begins to crack for white people in the "disintegration" phase; it typically happens when they develop a personal relationship that forces them to confront the relevance of race. This season of life may include a sense of discomfort, confusion, or guilt as the white person realizes his or her unearned advantages in a society that favors whiteness. If the white person chooses to courageously continue down the path of racial awareness, colorblindness eventually gives way to color-consciousness.

In the book *White Awake*, author and pastor Daniel Hill relates how he first encountered his racial identity as a white man. The journey began when he officiated the wedding of a friend who was of Indian descent. The wedding reflected his friend's Indian culture through the food, the clothing, and the music at the wedding. Hill remarked to his friend, "You have such an amazing culture! . . . I wish I had a culture too." It's easy to predict what comes next. "Daniel, you may be white," his friend said. "But don't let that lull you into thinking you have no culture."[13] His friend's remark about white people having a culture stuck with Hill, and he began learning more about the reality of race and its past and present reality in the United States. A brief comment from a friend became a pivotal step in his journey from colorblindness to color-consciousness.

Following the contact phase there may be a period called "reintegration" where a white person clings even more tightly to unhelpful racial ideas. They may blame people of color for their own hardships without accepting the fact that history, institutions, and policies continue to adversely impact racial and ethnic minorities while offering racial privileges to white people. Many people remain stuck in this phase. This is well reflected in the attitude of Tim Hershman, a white man from Akron, Ohio. "If you apply for a job, they seem to give the blacks the first crack at it," he responded to a poll question. "And, basically, you know, if you want any help from the government, if you're white, you don't get it. If you're black, you get it."[14]

Hershman seems to ascribe to the erroneous concept of "reverse racism," which is the idea that the effort to address historic racial inequities has led to racism against white people. It is clear that people of color may act in prejudicial ways against white people by judging them solely based on their skin color. But racism is more than an individual or interpersonal attitude. It includes systems, structures, and institutions owned and operated by those who hold the power to make decisions. As journalist and author Renni Eddo-Lodge explained it in her book *Why I'm No Longer Talking to White*

People about Race, "Everyone has the capacity to be nasty to other people, to judge them before they get to know them. But there simply aren't enough black people in positions of power to enact racism against white people on the kind of grand scale it currently operates against black people."[15]

Looking at economics and politics, two of the predominant seats of power in our nation today, it is clear that white people still occupy many of the positions of power. Nationwide, in 2018 about 40 percent of people identified as racial or ethnic minorities.[16] As of 2019, just four of the CEOs of *Fortune* 500 companies were Black (not including one black interim CEO). Only eleven were Latinos. Looking at the Boards of Directors of these companies, people of color held 16 percent of those seats.[17] In 2018, Sharice Davids of Kansas and Debra Haaland of New Mexico became the first two Native American women elected to the US House of Representatives.[18] No African American had served as a US Senator for a southern state since Reconstruction until Tim Scott was appointed to fill a vacancy in 2013.[19] The erroneous concept of "reverse racism" and the perception among some that white people have it harder in the United States because of race than people of color is a characteristic sign of people who have much further to go in their racial identity development.

White people who are able to productively handle their feelings of resistance to the idea of white privilege or the idea that racism still exists can progress to a phase called "pseudo-independence." In this stage of white racial identity development, people understand racism is an issue, and they seek out people of color to help them understand. But they primarily rely on others to do the work of fighting racism without recognizing their own ability—or responsibility—to be part of the solution.

At the most mature stage of white racial identity development, "autonomy," white people become allies and advocates for people of color. For every racial and ethnic group, individuals should be striving to recognize the ongoing importance of race in society today. Race and ethnicity can exert influence on where one is likely to live, how much a person makes at their job, which social networks they inhabit and the quality of the healthcare they receive. At the same time, race and ethnicity are not the only markers of identity. Someone who is productively engaging in their own racial identity development will always be aware that they are sons, daughters, spouses, workers, and believers. The goal for everyone is to have a positive view of their racial and ethnic identity, one that does not require assimilation or rejection of culture or experiences, and one that values the diversity of other people. Racially mature people will assert not only that their race is a factor in how they experience the world but also that identity is more than skin deep.

Write Your Racial Autobiography

The life of an enslaved person in the United States was never easy, but it was even harder for Black women. Born in North Carolina in 1813, Harriet Jacobs spent much of her life avoiding the sexual exploitation commonly endured by enslaved women. Her slave holder, a white man named Dr. Norcom, made his interest in raping her known while she was still a child. She spent years refusing his advances and chose instead to have children with a white lawyer who, she hoped, would free the children they had together. He did not. Finally, she escaped north to freedom, a journey that included seven years of hiding out in her grandmother's attic. Harriet Jacobs wrote down her life story and published it in a book called *Incidents in the Life of a Slave Girl*.[20]

For centuries Black people have told their own stories of oppression and pursuit of racial justice in a genre of literature known as the "slave narrative." These accounts revealed the hardship that characterized life for many enslaved and formerly enslaved Black people. Northerners and white people who would otherwise only hear misinformation about slavery read narratives like the one Jacobs produced and got a

picture of the injustice inherent in the "peculiar institution."
These autobiographical works instigated necessary conversations about racism and slavery and motivated a small number
of people to work for the abolition of slavery.

In a similar way, recounting your story of race, whether as a
member of a marginalized group or as a white person, can also
create the kind of positive agitation needed for substantive
change. One reason people struggle to talk productively about
race is because they have not examined their own stories.
A lack of awareness of your narrative around race will make
it harder to locate yourself on the racial identity development
spectrum. You may be oblivious to the racial traumas you
are carrying or the prejudices you harbor. Writing a racial
autobiography is one way to uncover formative experiences
around race and deliberately glean lessons and insights from
those experiences. A racial autobiography is a self-reported
account of your history with race, and its purpose is twofold:
to better understand your own story and to build empathy
for others.

There are no set rules for writing down your racial autobiography, but here are a few suggestions that may prove helpful. First, do your best to actually write your story down, by
hand or on a digital device. Writing your racial autobiography
forces you to replay your racial record, perhaps for the first
time. Writing down this story will dust off memories, similar
to the experience of unearthing an old picture from a shoebox
stashed beneath your bed. Writing also forces you to think
carefully about your words and how you want to express your
thoughts. As you decide how to describe your experiences in
writing, you will develop clearer ideas about them. Don't get
bogged down trying to craft eloquent prose. Stick-figures of
thoughts can always be fleshed out later.

Writing is also shareable. You may want to let close friends
or family members read your racial autobiography . . . or not.
Maybe you will publish it on a blog or even in a book. But you
should not feel any pressure to share your story. Writing a

racial autobiography is mainly for your development, and it will be useful whether anyone ever sees it or not.

To spur your thinking, ask yourself the following questions:

- What is my earliest memory of race?
- Have I had any negative experiences associated with my racial identity or that of someone else?
- When did I start growing racially conscious?
- From whom or in what period of life did I learn the most about race and diversity?
- Can I describe the different stages of racial identity development I've gone through and what made me aware of each?
- What concerns me about my racial past?
- What encourages me about my racial past?
- Why do I "do" racial justice? What is its purpose for me?

It's natural when writing about your history of racial experiences to reflect on the future as well. What do you want to be true about yourself when it comes to race and racism? How can you actively fight racism today? What will you do differently in light of what you have done before?

Famed writer Joan Didion started writing down her life experiences at five years old. Reflecting as an adult on the habit of keeping notebooks, she said, "I think we are well advised to keep on nodding terms with the people we used to be, whether we find them attractive company or not."[21] Writing a racial autobiography will be an emotional experience for many people. You may remember again a distressing encounter you had as a child. You may recall how your parents understood race and wince at the memory. You may realize how a comment you made years ago could have come across as racist. The record of our previous selves may not make "attractive company," but it is honest company. Until we tell the truth about our own racial lives, we will never be able to tell the truth about our collective racial dilemma.

Explore Your Family's Racial Identity

A branch of therapy called "family systems therapy" seeks to address issues of mental health from the perspective of family units. It recognizes that much of who we are as individuals is shaped in community, especially the family.

Exploring your racial identity would be incomplete without also delving into your family's past and present views and experiences with race. To explore your family's racial identity, you will need to do some research and have some honest conversations. You will also need to prepare yourself spiritually and emotionally for what you might find. You might feel shocked, saddened, or angered when you learn your family's racial narrative. In some cases, you may be encouraged as you realize how intentional parents or mentors have been in developing your racial awareness and fighting against racism. Perhaps you'll find helpful patterns in your life and experiences that you can teach others and more consciously apply in your own interactions with different people.

In many Black families and families of color, older generations do not talk about the discrimination they faced. Doing so may bring up feelings of trauma and shame that can evoke an emotional and even a physiological response. In some cases, family members may not want to talk about incidents of racism because they want to shield others in their family from feeling the same pain they endured. In white families, there may also be feelings of guilt or shame associated with what racist family members did or believed. Yet unearthing these stories, with proper sensitivity and care, is essential to understanding your racial identity.

You might begin by looking at old family photos. Try to identify who is in each picture. Do you know where they lived and in what era? Did they immigrate to the country? From where? You may consider talking to siblings about race or racist attitudes in your family. They may remember incidents or feelings that you do not, and their knowledge can round out your recollections. Parents, grandparents, and other relatives should also be consulted, but bear in mind that you may meet reluctance or resistance.

Be honest about your purpose. Tell people that you are trying to understand your racial history and identity better, and to do that you want to understand how the people who influenced you think about such topics. The goal is to gather information, not necessarily to tell them what you think. Ask open-ended questions such as, "What was it like growing up in your family?" or "What do you remember about what was happening in your town when you were a teenager?" Listen without offering your own analysis or judgment. Even if you find the stories repugnant or painful, your willingness to listen will encourage more conversation.

In discovering your family's racial background, you will learn more about what you believe about race and why. You will more easily see how communities can contribute to helpful or harmful ideas about race. And you will become more aware of how you can encourage those closest to you to take intentional steps toward racial justice.

How to Teach Kids about Race

A corollary to learning about racial history is teaching your kids about the past and present reality of race. Race is already a difficult enough subject among adults. How do you talk about it with kids? Whether you are a schoolteacher, a parent, a relative, or a friend, you may encounter a child who has questions or experiences around race. Those occasions often come unexpectedly—after a day at school, in the middle of a television program, at the dinner table. In those moments, your response can either move the child further along the journey of racial justice or cause them to stumble. The stakes are high as we train up our children to value everyone and treat people with dignity. You won't be able to adequately respond as an adult if you haven't already thought through how you might teach children about race.

The first step in teaching kids about race is teaching

yourself. You cannot appropriately respond to someone else's questions about race if you have not asked and attempted to answer your own. This is an added motivation to build up your racial awareness. Learning what the Bible says about how to treat people who are different and exploring your own racial autobiography are crucial elements that will help you respond in the right ways. You've taken an important step on the journey by reading this book. Just remember that the more you increase your capacity around issues of race and racism, the better you will be able to teach young people about the topic.

Teaching kids about race is similar in some ways to teaching kids about sex. Sex and sexuality are delicate topics that are personal and fraught with confusion and the potential for harm. At the same time, they are far too important not to discuss. If adults avoid teaching kids sexual ethics, then kids will likely get their information from potentially less helpful sources such as pop culture or their peers. The same is true regarding racial justice. It is incumbent on the adults who care about children to make sure they know as much as possible about how to be a gracious and compassionate adult, especially on the topic of race.

When talking to kids about race it is often necessary to push through your fears. *What if I say the wrong thing? What if I don't know the answer? What if I am replicating the racism I've seen or grown up with?* These questions are natural and unavoidable. You cannot go around them; you must push through them and talk about them. Bumbling through a conversation about race is often better than not having a conversation at all.

You must also realize that talking about race is not a one-time lecture but an ongoing dialogue. You cannot sit down and have *the* "race talk" with kids; you must have many "race talks." Knowing that you have multiple opportunities to talk to kids about race should also relieve some of the pressure. You do not need to cram every bit of necessary information into a single conversation. And if you happen to get something wrong or you later realize how you could have explained something better, don't worry; you may have the opportunity to revisit the dialogue at a later point.

You may not want to wait until a painful or confusing incident to talk about race with kids. Every conversation about race with kids has to start somewhere. You can even use the ARC of Racial Justice as a framework—awareness, relationship, and commitment. You don't have to use those exact terms, but the categories are helpful to make sure you give a thorough introduction and make it easy to remember. A hypothetical conversation with an elementary school age child about racial justice might go like this:

Have you ever noticed that people look different? Some are tall, some are short. Some have caramel skin or chocolate skin. These differences make life fun and never boring. But sometimes people do bad things, and we treat each other differently just because of how we look or where we come from, or how we talk. But there's something you can do about that. There are lots of things we can do to help people feel safe, valued, and loved.

Awareness: First, we need to learn about who they are. Instead of being scared of differences, we can celebrate them.

Relationships: We should also be excited about being friends with all different kinds of people. People who have different hair, clothes, food, and languages than we do. We might discover something new to like about the world, and people with lots of different friends do the best job of getting along with others.

Commitment: But just like you have rules in school, you'll have rules as a grown up too. Have you ever thought a rule was unfair? Just like people can be mean to each other, an unfair rule is kind of like being mean. As you get older you'll see lots of rules that seem unfair. The question is what are you going to do about it? If you see something wrong, you absolutely have the ability to raise your voice, take action, and try to change the rule. You won't always be able to make the changes you want, but it's trying that counts.

If you can remember to learn about people, have lots of different kinds of friends, and work together for change, then you'll be someone who helps make the world a better place.

The basic outline of this conversation would remain the same for older kids, but you can use different vocabulary and add more complex examples. For children of any age, connecting abstract conversations about race to the real world—memories, trips they've taken, books they've read, current events—is usually a good practice.

But we can't just talk to kids about race; we have to "show" them about race too. When learning how to multiply in grade school, you may remember your teacher pulling out "base ten blocks." They were little cubes arranged in rows of ones, tens, or hundreds designed to make the abstract principle of multiplication understandable through the use of tangible objects. In a similar way, a child learning about race may find the concept confusing when it is only described using words. Adults can help children understand race, and more importantly racial justice, by using concrete examples and experiences.

Visuals can help a child better understand race. A box of crayons with its many colors can show a child the value of variety. Drawing pictures would get boring very quickly if we only had one or two colors, but the rainbow of colors makes pictures vivid and pleasing. Going to the physical site of a place that has an important story to tell about racial justice or injustice can help too. You can read historical markers aloud, walk around the building or the location, learn about the place online beforehand, and use the entire experience as a conversation catalyst.

The best conversations about race intersect organically with what a child experiences regularly in his or her world. Whether it comes from a comment a character on a cartoon made or an interaction at the grocery store, pausing in the moment or soon thereafter to talk about race makes such conversations feel normal and regular.[22] Using the culture, spaces, and relationships kids encounter every day is one of the most effective ways to teach kids about race. Once you start looking, you'll find that the problem is not finding opportunities to talk about race with young people; it's having more than you ever expected.

Create a Pipeline of Mental Health Therapists of Color

I am a big proponent of mental health care through professional therapy. During the novel coronavirus pandemic in 2020, I started using an online service for therapy. In the first conversation with the therapist assigned to me, I could tell that she did not have the racial awareness to help me cope with the issues of racism I deal with constantly. Thankfully I was able to switch therapists, and my second therapist was a Black woman who understood both personally and professionally how to treat the wounds of racism.

Racial trauma is contextual and specific. It derives from the particular characteristics and social experiences connected to social meanings that one's race or ethnicities carry. These wounds are so particular that it can be hard for a white person to understand and effectively treat clients of color who have mental health issues related to their experience of racism. More than simply an issue of demographic diversity, there is the challenge of preparing therapists to serve a diverse racial and ethnic clientele, and this affects their training and curriculum. "The [mental health] field has ethnocentrically assumed that the material taught in traditional mental health programs is equally applicable to all groups."[23] The paucity of therapists from racial and ethnic minority groups, along with a lag in culturally responsive training materials, means there is an urgent need to diversify both the demographics and curricula of the mental health profession.

Of course, this does not mean that white therapists cannot effectively work with people of color. With enough study, experience, and empathy, therapists can serve clients from a variety of racial and ethnic backgrounds. But according to Pew Research Center's "Race in America 2019" survey, a person's race has a significant impact on their personal identity, and that's certainly true for therapists too. The Pew survey indicates that 84 percent of Black Americans named racial discrimination as a major reason for why it is harder for Black people to achieve compared to 54 percent of white respondents. People of color are more likely to see race as a central part of their identity. Of Hispanics and Asians, 59 percent and 54 percent of each group respectively cited race as a key component of their identity. At 74 percent, Black people were the most likely to highlight race as core to their identity. Just 15 percent of white respondents said race is important for how they think about themselves.[24]

Because white people and people of color think about and experience race differently, white people often do not have the experiential or clinical backgrounds to make them the best candidates for addressing the unique pains of racism. All therapists will have to work hard to treat mental health issues arising from instances of racism, but white therapists may have to work even harder.

One way to alleviate the adverse effects racism has on mental health and bridge the cultural gap between therapists and clients is to create a pipeline of therapists of color. Becoming a licensed therapist requires an undergraduate degree and usually an advanced degree, hundreds of hours of practical experience, and the ability to pass the standardized tests for certification. These milestones help ensure that the people who treat people's mental health are qualified to do so, but they can also pose obstacles to people of color entering the profession.

An article in *Psychology Today* notes, "Racial/ethnic minorities represent 30 percent of the population, yet 83.6 percent of mental health professionals identify as non-Hispanic Whites." The articles goes on to state that "in 2013, only 5.3 percent of psychologists were African Americans," and even today, only 5 percent of students enrolled in graduate-level psychology programs are Black.[25] Why are there so few people of color in the mental health field? The reasons are many. There are stigmas in some communities about admitting mental health illnesses and seeking professional help. Since many racial and ethnic minorities also face hardships due to financial poverty, cost is another factor. And the lack of racial and ethnic diversity in mental health fields may also make it harder for people of color to see it as a viable professional pathway for them.

We need more therapists of color. Creating funding, mentoring, and professional opportunities can help develop a pipeline of people of color who enter psychology, counseling, and related fields. Churches and community organizations can pool funds to create scholarships for students of color who want to go to college or graduate school to become professional mental health practitioners. In addition, societies created to support and advance therapists of color, such as the Association of Black Psychologists, already exist and should be supported. You or your church could contribute to scholarship funds for people of color interested in getting trained in mental health and therapy. In addition, pastors and other church leaders can help remove the stigma of therapy by preaching and teaching about the importance of getting mental health care and by talking about their own experiences with counseling. If you or someone you know is a mental health professional of color, consider establishing or joining mentorship or internship programs to train up a new generation of therapists and counselors. Bring in therapists and counselors of color to your church or workplace to talk about the unique issues of racial trauma and identity. Representation is important and seeing someone in the mental health profession who reflects your racial or

ethnic identity helps you envision yourself in a similar occupa-
tion. Diversity in a professional field does not guarantee that
people of color receive more or better treatment, but creating a
pipeline of mental health professionals who are people of color
could provide the possibility that more people suffering from
racial trauma will seek and get the help they need.

The ARC of Racial Justice encourages us to build our
awareness not just of society but our own souls. Many people
assume they know what they believe about race and racism
and why they believe it, so the assumption goes unexamined.
By taking the steps to reflect on our experiences with race,
we can better understand our attitudes on the topic. It takes
support, reflection, and resilience to unpack your racial history, but doing so will make you a more effective advocate for
racial justice.

Chapter 4

HOW TO STUDY THE HISTORY OF RACE

In his piercingly insightful essay, "Unnameable Objects, Unspeakable Crimes," James Baldwin reflected on the importance of history. Baldwin explained, "For history, as nearly no one seems to know, is not merely something to be read. And it does not refer merely, or even principally, to the past. On the contrary, the great force of history comes from the fact that we carry it within us, are unconsciously controlled by it in many ways, and history is literally present in all that we do."[1] History is alive.

In order to effectively fight racism, we must learn from the past. Contrary to the popular saying, historians are quick to point out that history does not, in fact, repeat itself. Historical events are too circumstantial and too contingent on a multitude of factors, decisions, actors, and conditions to ever simply repeat. But history does rhyme. We can hear cadences and syncopations of the past in the present. Learning about history is more than learning about what has happened before, it is about understanding what is happening now.

In this chapter, I want to address the need to develop a greater awareness of race as it has played out in your broader community, nation, and the world. This builds on the work you did in the previous chapter of writing your racial autobiography. Although your experiences contain deep wells of wisdom to inform your journey in pursuit of racial justice, this is not the only kind of knowledge you will need. This is a point that people of color need to hear as well. If you have endured racism or discrimination because of your racial or ethnic identity, then you have important and indispensable experiential knowledge about the ways racism functions. But individual experiences are necessarily limited. Learning about the history of race is a task for everyone.

Essential Understandings

Why Study History?

History is context. In seminary, my professors taught me that in order to read the Bible effectively you must know the context of the part of the Bible you are reading. I learned to ask whether the passage is poetry or narrative, who the authors were, when they were writing and to whom. What were the sociocultural conditions at the time, and what did the words mean in the original Hebrew, Aramaic, or Greek language? All of this is important to help readers "rightly divide the word of truth," and the same is true when it comes to learning history.

To learn history is to learn context. As historians often say, "Everything has a history," and that includes issues of racial justice. Like the men of Issachar in the Bible who "understood the times" (1 Chron. 12:32), if you want to understand the present, you must first understand the past.

When a white police officer killed Mike Brown, a Black teenager, and made #BlackLivesMatter a national rallying cry, I, like many others, sought to understand the situation. How did a predominantly white police force come to patrol a predominantly Black neighborhood? Why was the community of Ferguson so segregated in the first place? As I endeavored to understand our present-day context, I found that historians often had the most helpful information. They explained the history of red-lining and restrictive covenants that relegated

Black people to certain neighborhoods. They talked about the origins of the police force and their connections to slave patrols. I learned from historians that the past is a key to understanding and fighting racism today.

We need to study history not simply to know more about the past but to know more about ourselves. History is about identity. Rightly remembering our communal stories is a way of situating ourselves within a broader narrative. History tells us who and where we come from, how the people and events before us have shaped who we are now, and what kind of actions we need to take in order to pursue a more racially just future. Without a sense of history we lose our sense of self.

Ad Fontes

During the Protestant Reformation of the sixteenth century, the Latin phrase *ad fontes*—back to the sources—became a rallying cry. The Reformers urged a renewed emphasis on reading biblical texts in the original Greek, Hebrew, and Aramaic languages—not someone else's interpretation of them—in order to better understand Scripture.[2] The emphasis on primary sources is also a key tenet of doing good history.

Learning about the history of race potentially has transformative power because it shows not simply what people believed or aspired to but what they actually did. Although historical analysis always involves interpretation, the raw materials of history are facts, and the foundation for any good historical examination comes from primary sources—the evidence left behind by historical actors themselves. Primary sources can take the form of documents, speeches, songs, journals, interviews, newspapers, physical objects, and much more. It is the factual basis of history that makes it so effective in understanding race.

A Pew Research survey from 2011, 150 years after the Civil War began, showed that 48 percent of respondents thought the Civil War was about "states' rights" compared to 38 percent who thought it was about slavery.[3] In attributing the war to states' rights, people mean that the Confederate states did not go to war with the Union because they wanted to preserve slavery but because they protested the supposed interference of the federal government in state-level affairs. But if the war was about states' rights, then we have to ask, "What did the states want the right to do?" Primary sources help answer this question.

South Carolina led the way as the first state to secede from the Union. The state cited northern states' increasing antislavery sentiments, particularly their reluctance to enforce laws related to returning escaped slaves to their former masters, as cause for separation. "But an increasing hostility on the part of the non-slaveholding States to the institution of slavery, has led to a disregard of their obligations. . . . Thus the constituted compact has been deliberately broken and disregarded by the non-slaveholding States, and the consequence follows that South Carolina is released from her obligation."[4] The enforcement of laws concerning slavery provided the direct impetus for South Carolina to secede.

Similarly, the Mississippi Articles of Secession explain the reasons why the state's leaders decided to withdraw from the Union and join the Confederacy, and they clearly tie their concerns to slavery. "Our position is thoroughly identified with the institution of slavery—the greatest material interest of the world. Its labor supplies the product which constitutes by far the largest and most important portions of commerce of the earth."[5]

Alexander Stephens, the vice president of the Confederate States of America, outlined the ethos of the rebellious states. In his famous "Cornerstone Speech" given in March 1861, he said the Confederacy's "cornerstone rests upon the great truth, that the negro is not equal to the white man, that slavery— subordination to the superior race—is his natural and normal condition."[6] Within the context of these primary sources, you could certainly say that Confederate states seceded for states' rights—but only if you mean the supposed right of states to decide whether they would allow white people to own Black people. An awareness of history derived from primary sources makes it easier to dismantle the myths and untruths we still encounter today.

The remainder of this chapter offers suggestions for how to develop an awareness about history as it relates to race. These are practices that will help you understand the context necessary for identifying and fighting racism in the present-day.

Racial Justice Practices

Learn from Academic Historians

If you visit the history section of many brick and mortar bookstore chains, you might get the impression that the general public is only interested in military campaigns, presidents, and biographies of the rich, famous, and notorious. There is, of course, much more to know about history than what we generally find in commercial bookstores. Often, if we wish to delve deeper into the history of race, we must learn from academic historians. These men and women have dedicated their careers to the careful study of the past. They have spent incalculable hours in the stacks at libraries poring over thousands of documents in the archives and in lonely offices pondering how to make sense of the past. Academic historians must also subject their work to peer review where other experts in the field examine their research to offer critique and correction, so the resulting work is a collaborative effort that has been vetted through the professional standards of an academic discipline. It can easily take a scholar a decade or more of research, writing, and revision to compose a single monograph. All of this means you will typically find more detailed and well-attested information from academic historians than the popular history found on the shelves of large bookstore chains.

To learn from academic historians, you should first determine your areas of interest. What time period do you want to learn about? What nation or community? What aspect of history—gender, race, class, politics, culture? Look for books from university presses: for example, University of Illinois Press, University of Kentucky Press, and Princeton University Press. These publishers focus on publishing texts from scholars whose work has undergone rigorous preparation and revision.

While academic publishing has a reputation for being dry and inaccessible to those outside the field, there's good news: Academic historians have been making their work increasingly accessible to the public. *Black Perspectives* is a blog that is "deeply committed to producing and disseminating cutting-edge research that is accessible to the public and is oriented towards advancing the lives of people of African descent and humanity."[7] Sponsored by the African American Intellectual Historical Society, they have published hundreds of articles from top scholars about nearly every facet of Black history, both national and international. Columns such as "Made by History" at the *Washington Post* demonstrate the commitment of some national news outlets to provide their readers with the historical context necessary to understand current events.[8] The popularity of podcasts such as *Backstory* and documentaries such as *13th* and *I Am Not Your Negro* attest to the current hunger for history among the general population. All of these resources have been composed or informed by historians who know the content better than anyone else. This is not about only listening to people with PhDs. Useful knowledge can come from people with a variety of educational backgrounds and qualifications. Racial justice means learning racial history from those most informed about it.

How to Spot Trustworthy History

The discipline of history, even in its most scholarly forms, is more than the assemblage of facts. The data requires interpretation and opinion. What topics people choose, what questions they ask, what access they have to resources, how they choose to arrange the facts, and what meaning they give to historical events all depend on subjective reasoning. Historian Kevin Gannon describes the myth of objectivity in the writing of history: "But the idea of an objective version of history-telling, from which all others are deviant, is an absurdity. There is no objectivity in History. The very act of selecting a topic, for example, is privileging certain facts—making them 'historical'—over others."[9] This implies that all historical treatments hold some sort of bias. This is not necessarily a bad thing as long as you know history-telling has an element of subjectivity. If all history has some sort of slant and is subject to factual error, then how do you know which history to trust?

First, as stated above, you should seek out primary sources. The best way to verify the facts and to decide for yourself what they mean is to go to the original documents. In this digital age, institutions make all kinds of historical documents available online. If you want to know exactly what Stokely Carmichael (Kwame Ture) said in a speech, you can explore the SNCC Digital website. If you want to know what articles editors chose for the first issue of *Christianity Today* magazine in 1956, you can subscribe to the magazine and search the archives for yourself. You can search issues of the *New York Times* all the way back to the nineteenth century on their website. Every state has some sort of official repository of archives and history. Colleges and universities also house specific collections, such as Stanford University's Martin Luther King Jr. Research and Education Institute, which contains the most extensive collection of King's papers. If you cannot find an original source, then there is good reason to be skeptical of the data. Going to the primary sources enables you to see for yourself the exact words or images related to a particular historical event or person. You can also gauge the accuracy of secondary sources, those analyses that rely on primary sources, by going to the original documents as much as possible.

Second, you should rely on multiple sources for historical data. Cross-check information with several sources to see if there's a consensus. While researching for another project,

I found a powerful and incriminating quote that I wanted to use to make a point about racism in politics. But I had to verify its accuracy first. I read the quote in a news article. Then I traced the quote to a book. The book referenced an audio interview—a primary source—which I was then able to find online. Sure enough, there was the quote stated by the subject himself. But I had to track it down across three different platforms to be sure I had it right. If an event has been deemed historically significant, it is likely that others will have agreed and written or otherwise communicated about it. Do your best to verify facts by comparing multiple sources.

Finally, be wary of any history that casts the story of humanity as one of inevitable progress with clear heroes and villains. In 1931, British historian Herbert Butterfield wrote a book called *The Whig Interpretation of History*. Named after one of the two major political parties in Britain during the 1700s and 1800s, a whiggish interpretation of history "comes into play whenever history is written either by, or on behalf of, a triumphant elite."[10] Simplistic narratives that pit champions of progress against ideologically backward and morally questionable opponents usually obscure more than they reveal. Was victory in World War II an unmitigated triumph? Not according to the victims of the atomic bombs dropped on Hiroshima and Nagasaki or those who feared nuclear war. Were the cowboys the "good guys" and the Native Americans the "bad guys?" Not if you view it from the perspective of the indigenous inhabitants.

Where we find ourselves in the present day is the result of complex and competing forces that evade linear narratives of progress. The line between good and evil is not always clear. Search for the histories that honor the complexity of the human experience.

Learn Your Local History

One of the best places to start learning about the history of race is right where you are. Important history is all around us, but the significance of what happened nearby can sometimes be lost because familiarity leads to invisibility. Sometimes we grow so accustomed to seeing our surroundings that we have to rediscover how to interrogate our environment to glean lessons from the local past.

Spoken word artist Propaganda is featured in a song called "Gangland" by Lecrae. In just a few words, he explains what's in a name.

> There's a high school in Alabama named after Robert
> E. Lee
> And it's eighty-nine percent black, you don't see
> the irony?
> What it do to a psyche, it's simple, you don't like me . . .

Of course, Robert E. Lee was a general in the Confederate Army during the Civil War and became one of the most celebrated cultural icons in the myth of the Lost Cause—a narrative that characterizes the Confederacy as a noble endeavor to preserve "the Southern way of life" against the agitation of northerners and Black people. It created legendary heroes and despised villains. The Lost Cause is still salient today, as the Confederacy and its champions invoke a nostalgic past to which some people wish to return. For instance, naming a high school after Lee, a man who fought to defend race-based chattel slavery is, in itself, disturbing, but when the school's population is also overwhelmingly Black, the act is an insult.

Have you ever wondered who or what a place was named after? Names surround us—on street signs, buildings, counties, and cities. Names matter. They explain part of a community's history, who gets to tell that history, and what they value. The names in your community communicate volumes about its history. Names like Arapahoe County, Missisquoi River, and Mohegan Elementary School reveal a hard truth about cities across the United States. From the most populous metropolises on the coasts to the rolling prairies of the heartland, Native Americans were here first, and we are on their land.

In 2015, Mark Charles, a man of Navajo and Dutch American descent, walked up to a group of people assembled for a Columbus Day celebration and said, "You cannot discover lands already inhabited." In a book he cowrote called *Unsettling Truths*, Charles explained that he repeated the sentence again and again getting louder each time until he finally arrived at the front of the group. "Suck it up," said one of the white men gathered to celebrate the occasion. Eventually one of the participants grabbed Charles's arm and roughly escorted him away saying, "You're not welcome here." The people who gathered to celebrate Columbus that day may not have wanted to hear what Mark Charles had to say, but his point must be amplified and repeated.[11]

Contrary to the trite history lessons many of us learned, Christopher Columbus did not "discover" North America. These lands already had a diverse and storied population of indigenous inhabitants. The United States exists on land stolen from Native Americans. As people concerned about racial justice grapple with the contradiction of living in the "Land of Liberty" that was built on the displacement and murder of Native Americans, one proactive measure we can take is to learn who the original inhabitants were and where they are now. Several tools now exist to remind us of who originally lived on the land we currently occupy.[12] If you go online, you can find interactive maps that allow you to enter an address or a zip code, and it will tell you which nations originally lived on the land in that area. Beyond simply knowing the name of the nation, you can go further by learning its history. What language did they speak? What treaties or wars led to their displacement? What is the state of the nation in the present day?

As a small but public gesture, some speakers begin their events by acknowledging the nation that once lived on the land. Reminding people about the Native Americans, the

indigenous people of North America, through formal proc-
lamations and in casual discussions helps develop a sense of
humility by acknowledging that most people in North America
benefit from the theft of Native land. We are all implicated in
injustice.

Take Them Down

Black activists had been objecting to the presence of four
Confederate monuments in the city of New Orleans for years
before Mitch Landrieu, the former Mayor of New Orleans,
added his voice in 2015 to a multiyear effort to remove them.
Still, against much opposition, the last of four monuments
came down in 2017, and Landrieu gave a speech to mark the
occasion.

He began in the right place, with the original inhabitants
of the land on which New Orleans stands. He named "the
Choctaw, Houma Nation, the Chitimacha. Of Hernando De
Soto, Robert Cavelier, Sieur de La Salle, the Acadians, the
Islenos," and more. He went on to discuss the city's history as a
major slave port responsible for the trade of scores of Africans.
He spoke of the 540 known lynchings in the state of Louisiana.
Then he asked "why there are no slave ship monuments, no
prominent markers on public land to remember the lynchings
or the slave blocks; nothing to remember this long chapter of
our lives."[13]

Landrieu contrasted the absence of monuments commemorating Black history and resilience with the presence of
Confederate monuments. He did not see them as innocent,
benign, or patriotic symbols. "These monuments purposefully celebrate a fictional, sanitized Confederacy; ignoring
the death, ignoring the enslavement, and the terror that it
actually stood for." For that reason as well as the need to bring
healing to a racially divided city and state, he said, "We have
to reaffirm our commitment to a future where each citizen is
guaranteed the uniquely American gifts of life, liberty and the
pursuit of happiness."[14] Landrieu was right and communities

nationwide can learn from the determination and ingenuity he and his supporters exhibited in the face of vitriolic opposition.

Racial justice requires removing monuments that honor racist individuals and white supremacy. In dozens of cities around the United States, and not just in the South, emblems of the Confederacy pockmark the public landscape. They fly in the form of flags or stand as stone statues and monuments. These monuments and symbols should come down as a gesture that communities are moving in the right direction on the path of racial justice. One concrete action you can take is to find out who your state honors in the National Statuary Hall Collection. Each state donates two statues that honor people significant in the history of their state. Too often these women and men stood for slavery, segregation, and racism. The state of Mississippi, for example, honors Jefferson Davis, the president of the Confederate States of America. They also honor James Zachariah George, one of the men who signed the Mississippi Articles of Secession quoted earlier in this chapter. George is also known as the architect of the 1890 Mississippi Constitution which served as a template for Black voter disfranchisement. Who does your state honor? Will you lobby members of your state legislature to remove and replace racists?[15]

Some people object to removing Confederate iconography. They argue that taking them down is akin to erasing history. As a student of history, preserving tangible artifacts from the past is very important to me. But there are many ways to do that without giving the impression that our communities celebrate slavery or honor the individuals who did. At the University of Mississippi, students and sympathetic faculty and staff successfully lobbied for the removal of the Confederate statue that has stood at the main entrance of campus since 1906 to the much more secluded Confederate cemetery that is the final resting place of the university's students who died fighting in the Civil War.[16] Others have suggested putting the monuments into museums where they can be viewed in historical context.[17] Another suggestion some have proposed, especially for buildings named after slaveholders and segregationists, is putting up plaques that explain the person's beliefs and current efforts to move beyond such legacies and learn from the mistakes of the past.[18] There's a difference between veneration and remembrance. We should remember the past, even the most painful parts, but that does not mean we need to venerate those aspects of our history.

Another objection some have is that whatever Confederate symbols may have meant in the past, their connotation now is more positive. "Heritage not hate" is the refrain often invoked in the defense of Confederate iconography. The problem with "heritage not hate" as a defense of contemporary Confederate symbolism is that insofar as the Confederacy existed to defend race-based chattel slavery, its heritage *is* hate. It is the hatred of freedom, of the image of God in Black people, and of unity. There is much to celebrate about the culture and traditions prevalent in the southern United States—Blues music, catfish, Margaret Walker Alexander, and much more.[19] Why represent a region and a culture whose heritage you appreciate with the most reprehensible aspect of that place? For Christians, Scripture teaches us, "Do nothing out of selfish ambition or vain conceit. Rather, in humility value others above yourselves" (Phil. 2:3). Selfishness says, "This symbol represents heritage not hate to me, even though it represents terror and dehumanization to others." Humility says, "Whatever attachments I may have to Confederate symbols and monuments, I value others enough to consider their pain over my pride."

Monuments and symbols are about memory—how we choose to remember the past. They are about who gets included and who gets left out of our narratives. For too long people invested in white supremacy have inscribed the celebration of whiteness and denigration of people of color into our public landscapes. Fighting racism means honoring what is honorable. As a nation, we have literally put racists on pedestals while claiming to be committed to liberty and justice for all. A minimum requirement for racial progress is to remove the statues and symbols of racism and to replace them with commemorations of those who fought for the dignity and equality of all people.

Conduct an Oral History

On July 17, 2020, two leaders of the Civil Rights movement both died. Congressman John Lewis had been fighting for racial justice since the 1960s on the streets and in the nation's capital, and Rev. C. T. Vivian was one of the Freedom Riders who worked to end segregation and spent his life preaching and organizing for racial progress.[20] Today, we are living during the final years of the lives of participants in the Civil Rights movement. Even the youngest of these participants are now in their seventies and eighties. What will happen when this last generation of eyewitnesses passes from the earth? What questions will remain unanswered? Who will inspire the next generation of racial justice activists?

We cannot prolong anyone's life indefinitely, but we can honor their stories by inviting them to recount and record those narratives. This is the purpose of oral history. The Oral History Association says oral history is "a method of gathering, preserving and interpreting the voices and memories of people, communities, and participants in past events."[21] Before human beings created written language, they passed down stories of their families and communities through oral histories. In West African tradition, the griot (pronounced GRE-o) was a person responsible for remembering and sharing stories. They would communicate through poetry and song, and their role was invaluable in preserving the history and heritage of a people. We need modern-day griots who will take the responsibility to record and share the oral recollections of people.

As an academic discipline, oral historians have extensively taught and written about how to responsibly and respect-fully gather the recollections of others. The Southern Oral

History Project (SOHP) at the University of North Carolina, for instance, utilizes the academic study of oral history to "preserve the voices of the southern past." The Library of Congress contains an array of oral history projects that are digitized and searchable. These collections and others offer examples of professionally collected and archived oral histories.

Your efforts to discover oral histories need not be professional or academic, but they should still be collected and recorded conscientiously. Oral history is first and foremost an ethical endeavor. You must honor the people behind the stories. At the most basic level, taking an oral history means you cannot share anyone's story without their express permission. Even if meant only for your own personal use, you must tell the person your intentions.

Certain best practices are also associated with collecting and sharing an oral history. You must clearly identify your purpose. Are you attempting to find information about your family? Is this intended for a church or other religious community? What do you intend to do with the information? Ask informed questions. Come to the conversation having already done your homework so you know what questions to ask. Do not waste the interviewee's time fumbling with questions they cannot answer or trying to come up with queries on the spot. When possible, send the questions beforehand so people have time to think and even collect tangible artifacts. Ask open-ended questions such as:

- What was school like growing up?
- What was your first job?
- Can you describe the racial climate where you grew up?
- Did you grow up in a religious community? What did the people around you communicate about race?
- Do any incidents around race stand out to you?

A resource from the University of California at Los Angeles (UCLA) advises, "In general, think of the various topics of your interview as structured like an inverted pyramid: broad, general questions first, followed by follow-up questions that ask for more detail."[22] The goal is to collect narratives to better understand the historical context of a community through the lens of a particular person. These histories can add indispensable information that you cannot find online or in books to round out other facts and data.

Conduct an Institutional History

In 2014, the President's Commission on Slavery and the University at the University of Virginia organized a group of other Virginia colleges and universities that had all decided to study their institution's historic connections to slavery. This original group soon expanded beyond a single state and became the Universities Studying Slavery Consortium (USS). The USS "allows participating institutions to work together as they address both historical and contemporary issues dealing with race and inequality in higher education and in university communities as well as the complicated legacies of slavery in modern American society."[23] Such initiatives serve as models for any institution that wishes to examine its racial past.

All institutions that are serious about racial justice should examine their own organizational histories. Remembrance and repair begin at home. Communities and organizations need to explore their own ties to racism and white supremacy in order to have the integrity necessary to speak about racial justice today. They must go back and do the hard work of making restitution and repair for their own acts of injustice before moving forward with any visions for a racially just future. The Universities Studying Slavery group displays the power of working in collaboration with other institutions engaged in similar work of examining their racial past. The group hosts several symposia where institutions can share best practices and their journeys of transformation as they "unearth and understand" their racial past.[24] Churches, denominations, and other religious institutions can use the same collaborative approach to conduct their own institutional histories and move further down the path of racial justice.

How to Commemorate Juneteenth

In the days before the internet and email, news tended to travel slowly. It wasn't until June 19, 1865—a full two months after Robert E. Lee surrendered his Confederate Army to Union forces and two years after the Emancipation Proclamation—that enslaved Black people in Texas heard that the Civil War had ended and that their emancipation would soon be a reality. In the wake of the announcement, Black people erupted into celebration. The long night of their enslavement was finally giving way to the bright dawn of freedom.

Juneteenth, a portmanteau consisting of the words "June" and "nineteenth," stands as the oldest celebration of Black emancipation in the United States. To this day, the occasion marks the progress of the United States from legally approving race-based chattel slavery to legally abolishing it after centuries of resistance, the initiation of the nation's bloodiest war, and a constitutional amendment. Historically speaking, few events compare to the significance of the abolition of slavery in the United States. It forever changed the political and social landscape of the country. Yet our nation does relatively little to reflect its importance.

Setting aside Juneteenth as a day of remembrance, commemoration, and celebration would accomplish at least three goals. First, it would remind Americans that their country was birthed amid the idea and practice that white people could own Black people. The people of the United States would have an annual reminder of the great tragedy and incalculable suffering of millions that accompanied the establishment of the nation. Second, a national Juneteenth holiday would be an opportunity to celebrate progress. Emancipation was a massive step forward in the cause of racial justice. Many people sacrificed their lives in its pursuit. Freedom for the nearly four million Black people under slavery is a cause for rejoicing. Despite the many failures of the United States with regard to racism, there is still a need to pause to remember what has been accomplished. Third, celebrating Black emancipation would also remind us of the work that still needs to be done. In looking back at the history of slavery, people of the United States would have the chance to reflect on the "unfinished revolution" and consider ways to move forward.[25]

Most states have some form of recognition or commemoration on record, and some efforts have been made to make Juneteenth a national holiday.[26] But people in the United States can do more to recognize emancipation with greater intentionality. If you are able, plan a trip to coincide with Juneteenth and consider a visit to the National Museum of African American History and Culture in Washington, DC, or journey to Montgomery to visit the National Memorial to Peace and Justice dedicated to the victims of lynching. Historically, churches have served as Juneteenth celebration sites, and that tradition continues today. Gethsemane Church of God in Christ in Lafayette, Louisiana, has offered live gospel and jazz music, African drumming lessons, and a parade to commemorate the occasion.[27]

Local congregations or other groups can

- read a statement of commemoration during services,
- preach a sermon or record a special message on liberation,
- host Sunday school or Bible study lessons on history and liberation,
- bring in guest speakers (historians, preachers, community leaders, etc.),
- host a picnic or festival for the public, or
- offer a financial donation to a Black-led organization or a museum dedicated to Black history.

As the commemoration of Juneteenth becomes more common, white people should be careful not to appropriate the holiday from Black people. This happens when white people erase the suffering and brutality of slavery in favor of a celebratory message of perpetual progress. It also happens when white people fail to remember their historic role in racial injustice and celebrate as if they had nothing to do with the conditions that made Black emancipation necessary in the first place. The fact remains that white people practiced and defended race-based chattel slavery in the United States and this should be a cause for humble contrition. While it is a day of celebration for Black people, white people must rejoice along with Black people while also remembering the white supremacy their ancestors created and from which they still benefit. White people may consider supporting Black churches or organizations as they celebrate Juneteenth. They can host a teach-in for other white people to learn about slavery and its legacies. White people can also use it as a day to advocate for political and systemic changes that lead to racial equity. People of any race or ethnicity should commemorate Juneteenth, but do so with the appropriate reverence and humility.

William Faulkner said, "The past is never dead. It's not even past."[28] The ARC of Racial Justice reminds us that building our awareness necessarily includes learning more about the history of race and racism. The past unavoidably impacts the present. If we want to pursue racial justice today, then we need to know what happened in the past to create the circumstances of the present. History provides the vital context to pursue solutions that are rooted in a firm understanding in the causes and consequences of racism.

PART 2

RELATIONSHIPS

Chapter 5

HOW TO DO RECONCILIATION RIGHT

We sat on an assortment of couches, dining room chairs, and even coffee tables as we chit-chatted amiably but awkwardly in anticipation of that night's topic of conversation—race and the church. We were all members of the same intentionally multiracial congregation, and we had assembled following the murder of another unarmed Black person. I honestly, sadly, don't remember which specific incident because there are so many. But I do remember one particular story from that night.

A white husband and wife had befriended a Black husband and wife in the church. Each couple had children about the same age. Of course, their experiences had been vastly different because of race. As the group moved deeper into the dialogue, the white couple explained how they had learned what Black people meant by "the talk." One night when the Black and white couple were hanging out and socializing, the Black couple explained having "the talk" with their two teenage Black sons. The white couple had no clue what they were talking about. The Black couple went on to describe how they had to tell their sons how to survive being pulled over by the cops.

Turn on the dome light in the car if it's dark.
Don't make any sudden moves.
Keep your hands visible at all times.
Stay calm, no matter what the officer does.

All of this could mean the difference between an arrest, a beating, or even living or dying. The white husband told the group, "It never even crossed my mind to have that kind of talk with our white teenage sons." For both the white and the Black couple, it was a painful moment of revelation because it highlighted the different worlds their families inhabited. At the same time, it was a moment of greater unity and deeper friendship. They moved further along the journey of racial reconciliation, and it happened through relationships.

The Son of God becoming human in Jesus Christ—what theologians call the incarnation—demonstrates the truth that all reconciliation is relational. When God wanted to reconcile people to himself and to each other, he didn't send a tweet or a TikTok video; he sent his Son. Christ himself is the paradigm for our reconciliation efforts. God took on a human body. "The Word became flesh and made his dwelling among us" (John 1:14). The Bible reveals that God is not an abstract force but a personal and loving Creator who desires a relationship with the women, men, and children created in God's very image. But there's a problem.

Whenever we choose to rebel against God, we do not simply break a rule; we rupture a relationship. When we disobey the Creator, we create spiritual distance between us and God. We become our own little gods by creating rules for ourselves and defying the true and living God. The story of human history has been one of broken relationships between God and one another. Fortunately, God has a plan to reconcile all things.

We should be careful not to rush past the religious dimensions of reconciliation. Some people think they know the concept so well that they don't need to revisit it. Others are not especially religious and do not think religion is important to racial justice. To those who are familiar with the story, it always helps to hear it again from different perspectives. Why are there four gospels in the New Testament? They all tell essentially the same story, but from different viewpoints. The highlights and background of each gospel narrative reveal new aspects of familiar events. Word choice, detail, theme—all of these are expressed uniquely by different storytellers. So it is with the story of Christian reconciliation. Old truths can stand out in fresh ways when we hear them from new voices.

For those who do not consider themselves religious, one does not have to adhere to any particular religion to acknowledge the moral imperatives of reconciliation. Reconciling people across racial and ethnic boundaries reduces friction between groups, opens channels of communication and understanding, and moves communities toward inclusivity. The power of reconciliation holds true across times, places, and cultures. It transcends our natural tendencies toward self-centeredness in relationships and lead us to new heights of understanding others. But reconciliation with other people is not simply a matter of strategy, practices, and logical choices. It is a spiritual matter. Reconciliation needs a transcendent framework to serve as a guide on the journey toward racial justice, love, and wholeness. At a minimum, understanding religious, and specifically Christian, viewpoints on racial reconciliation will help you understand the operating principles that others hold. And understanding the problems of racial rupture at a spiritual level can aid attempts to bring healing.

This chapter begins the discussion of the "relationship" part of the ARC of Racial Justice. It considers the concept of reconciliation from a theological perspective. I believe one of the key tools in fighting racism is understanding the spiritual dimension of race relations. There is a divine morality that compels us to build or restore relationships with one another, and many of the racial justice practices highlighted here focus on what churches in particular can do to bring about reconciliation.

Essential Understandings

Racial Justice Often Begins with Relationships

As we have been learning, the mere accumulation of facts will not change the racial status quo. Nor will a commitment

to systemic change alone build bridges of interpersonal understanding. People need a personal motivation to disrupt the
regular patterns of racism in their own lives and in society.
Often it is a relationship or friendship that changes a person's
perspective. Reading a book about the Civil Rights movement
can be helpful, but hearing the grief in the voice of someone
who lived through it will leave a more lasting impression. It
is difficult to pursue effective structural remedies to racism
if you have little understanding of the personal experiences of
marginalized people. Relationships make reconciliation real
and motivate us to act.

Conciliation or Reconciliation?

Some will object to the very concept of reconciliation between
different racial and ethnic groups. "When have we ever been
at peace? When have we ever had a healthy relationship that
can be restored?" they will ask. Those are legitimate questions,
especially with regard to the long history of Black and white
people in the United States. Any study of history exposes the
lie that there was ever a placid era in which different racial
groups enjoyed warm peace and strong bonds. Some look back
with nostalgia to the 1950s when shows like *Leave it to Beaver*
seemed to represent the American people in a state of perfection—a nuclear family, a comfortable suburban home, a
breadwinning father, and a stay-at-home wife. In 1957, the
same year *Leave It to Beaver* premiered, US senator Strom
Thurmond of South Carolina engaged in the longest one-person
filibuster in history (over twenty-four hours) to oppose passage
of the Civil Rights Act of 1957.[1] Others may look with longing
to the "Roaring Twenties" and the days of flapper dancing
and the Harlem Renaissance. But in that decade Congress
passed the Immigration Act of 1924, which created quotas for
immigrants based on race and completely banned Japanese
immigrants for nearly thirty years. Yet others look with roman-
ticism upon the "Old West" of the nineteenth century. They
seldom know or tell the tales of the Indian Removal Act signed

into law by President Andrew Jackson in 1830. That act paved the way for the forcible removal of Native American nations east of the Mississippi River, such as the Cherokee, Chickasaw, Choctaw, and Muskogee.[2] Given the tumultuous history of race relations, the concept of reconciliation can seem as realistic as taking a running leap from Earth and touching the moon.

If different races of people have never had conciliation how can they have *re*-conciliation? One response is to ask, "How far back do you go?" In the Christian story before Genesis 3, there *was* harmony with God and between human beings. If it is possible to speak of reconciliation with God, then it is also possible to speak of reconciliation between people of different racial and ethnic groups.

On another level, however, reconciliation need not have anything to do with chronology or the search for a time or an era when people were at peace with one another. Perhaps reconciliation refers more fundamentally to the original pattern for relationships that must be restored and fulfilled. God created human beings to be at peace with one another and with God. The current state of relations between racial groups is often open war or, at best, a cold peace. Reconciliation does not mean returning to a bygone historical era of harmony but rather revising our relationships to more closely match God's foundational pattern for human interaction.

Reconciliation is a useful word in the journey of racial justice because it is a biblical word. Jesus has given his followers a message of reconciliation: "All this is from God, who reconciled us to himself through Christ and gave us the ministry of reconciliation" (2 Cor. 5:18). This is the great charge of Christians—to represent Christ's reconciliation in a world full of broken relationships. "We are therefore Christ's ambassadors, as though God were making his appeal through us. We implore you on Christ's behalf: Be reconciled to God" (2 Cor. 5:20). The disciples of Jesus Christ cannot abandon the word *reconciliation* because they cannot abandon the ministry of reconciliation.

The Problem with Racial Reconciliation

Yet even as it has gained in popularity, the concept of racial reconciliation has been drained of its transformational power in many circles. Since at least the mid-1990s, a variety of Christian groups and denominations have been vocal and enthusiastic about a certain form of racial reconciliation. In 1994, Black and white Pentecostals gathered for a conference in Memphis called "Pentecostal Partners: A Reconciliation Strategy for Twenty-First Century Ministry." Several presentations on the past, present, and future of racial reconciliation culminated in one white Pentecostal leader spontaneously washing the feet of a Black Pentecostal leader on stage in an act of contrition and repentance.[3]

In 1995, the Southern Baptist Convention, the largest Protestant denomination in the United States and one that was founded to preserve the so-called right of white Christians to hold slaves, finally repented of its racist origins. They passed a resolution on racial reconciliation that said, "We lament and repudiate historic acts of evil such as slavery from which we continue to reap a bitter harvest, and we recognize that the racism which yet plagues our culture today is inextricably tied to the past." It continued, "We hereby commit ourselves to eradicate racism in all its forms from Southern Baptist life and ministry."[4]

In 1996 the Promise Keepers movement, a ministry to Christian men that holds annual rallies for tens of thousands of people, chose racial reconciliation for its theme. They titled the rally "Break Down the Walls" based on Ephesians 2:14: "For he himself is our peace, who has made the two groups one and has destroyed the barrier, the dividing wall of hostility."[5] At one point in the conference, held at the Georgia Dome, the leader invited the pastors of color to come down to the floor of the arena. They encouraged other pastors to hug them on the way. "We hugged, patted and cheered for 45 minutes. It was wonderfully warm—warmed up the whole conference. There was a lot of crying," said one white pastor in attendance.[6]

At the end, many of the pastors who attended signed the "Atlanta Covenant," which had seven principles, one of which required, "Reaching beyond any racial and denominational barriers."[7]

Were these racial reconciliation efforts and similar ones effective? Perhaps. In 2012, Fred Luter became the first Black president of the Southern Baptist Convention. The percentage of churches considered "multiethnic"—where no single racial or ethnic group comprises more than 80 percent of the congregation—is on the rise. As of 2012, about 25 percent of Catholic churches were multiethnic, and the number of multiethnic Protestant churches tripled from 4 to 12 percent from 1998 to 2012.[8] These days it is not uncommon to find Black people and other racial and ethnic minorities represented among the leadership of historically white churches, denominations, missions agencies, and nonprofits of all kinds.

But racial reconciliation as it is popularly understood and practiced in evangelical Christian circles suffers from three main shortcomings: it misdiagnoses the problem as "separation," it does not properly address power dynamics, and it does not take gender into account.

How do evangelicals misdiagnose the problem? In evangelical circles, racism is often reduced to individual behaviors and attitudes. In this understanding, the forces that separate people of different races and ethnicities come from personal prejudice. An individualistic understanding of reconciliation presents racial separation as the problem. The solution, therefore, is to get people together. This leads to grand statements such as the Southern Baptist resolution against slavery or large one-time events aimed at reconciliation like the Promise Keepers rally in 1996. When evangelicals focus on bringing people together, they often leave out any analysis of the systemic and institutional forces that led to the separation in the first place. Occasional racial proximity is too low a goal for reconciliation.

Racial reconciliation as practiced in evangelical circles also fails to adequately address the issue of power. Power comes in many forms—economic, political, cultural, and more. In the United States, white people have and still hold much of the power, and this is true even in many churches and denominations. Current racial reconciliation efforts often fail to deal with the vectors of power. Who has the money? The ones with the money determine what programs to fund and which individuals get financial support in ministry. Who has positional authority? The people in positions of power actually get to decide the priorities and policies of the community.

Diversity in leadership is an absolute must-have if an organization desires diversity. But putting a token person of color on a leadership team does not ensure positive change. You may have desegregated your leadership team, but that does not mean you have an integrated team. Integration means incorporating diverse perspectives, people, and practices into an organization so that the culture expands to include diversity while maintaining unity. Desegregation simply means that people are not *excluded* from participation because of their race or ethnicity. Desegregation does not say anything about how racial and ethnic minorities are *included* in decision-making, how much power is shared with them, or how they are supported when exercising that power.

One form of power that can be difficult to identify is cultural power. "The exercise of power is not typically overt or mean-spirited but rather it is done in the name of cultural or theological unity."[9] Racial reconciliation must also address how power is mediated through culture. This should not be cultural assimilation where anyone different must adapt to the norms and preferences of the dominant group. In predominantly white settings, this brand of racial reconciliation fails to dismantle the practices that privilege white people and their cultural norms. What evangelical racial reconciliation often means for Black people and other people of color is leaving their own communities to join predominantly white churches, adhering to the preaching and musical styles of the majority group, and learning under mainly white leadership. This is not integration; it is assimilation.

Yet another way in which popular understandings of racial reconciliation fall short is in not addressing gender. Chanequa Walker-Barnes highlights this deficiency in her book, *I Bring the Voices of My People*. She tells us that "women—particularly women of color—have largely been invisible in the field of reconciliation."[10] In scanning the literature around racial reconciliation she finds mostly books by male authors. The results are approaches to reconciliation "that are less about ending racism than they are about ensuring that White men and men of color have equal access to male privilege."[11] Building a theology and practice of racial reconciliation that includes an analysis of gender from the start leads to a more holistic concept of reconciliation that is truly inclusive not just across racial and ethnic lines but gender lines as well. Although the focus of this book does not allow for an extended discussion of gender, we must not forget that race never operates in isolation from gender dynamics.

Despite these problems, racial reconciliation is still a worthy goal if we can recover its true definition. The following practices of reconciliation can help Christians and others to "do reconciliation right."

Racial Justice Practices

Incorporate Lamentation into Worship

If you have not learned to lament, you have not learned to love. To love someone is to know and be known, which means opening oneself up to the possibility of being hurt by another. In love, we leave ourselves vulnerable to the failings and flaws of others. When love is betrayed and people hurt others because of racial arrogance, it is cause for lament.

Those who have learned to lament will be able to sing their sadness. Blues music emerged in the Deep South, especially the Mississippi Delta, in the late nineteenth century, and it is known for its use of certain chords and notes called "blue notes" to express a mood of sadness and fatigue. The music grew out of the souls of Black folks as they picked cotton in the Jim Crow era of sharecropping. They sang of broken hearts, love lost, and the unfairness of life. Even though the themes spoke of life's difficulties, singing the blues was also cathartic. It expressed pain in the language of lyrics and melodies. The very act of singing or strumming that emotion helped strengthen the performers and the hearers for another day.

According to music lore, Robert Johnson sold his soul to the devil in exchange for his musical genius at the crossroads of highways 61 and 49 in his native Mississippi Delta. Although the story is apocryphal, one of Johnson's songs, "Hellhound on My Trail," speaks to the sense of being tailed by an enemy.[12] Recorded in 1937, the song echoes one of King David's psalms. Where David speaks of "dismay," Johnson speaks of the "blues"—different words for the same feeling. Johnson spoke of a "hellhound on my tail," and David wrote that "the enemy pursues me." Both shared the sense of being harassed and weary. Black Americans in the Jim Crow era could certainly relate to the sense of being hounded by injustice and exhausted by the travail of trying to survive in an unjust world.

Every community dedicated to racial justice should have a canon of songs devoted to lament. In fact, many psalms are lamentations meant to be sung in congregational worship. Songs of lamentation come in various musical styles, and congregations can discern what will best speak to them. The important part is that we include the full spectrum of human emotion, including "the blues," in our worship. When we express lament through song, it has a way of lifting the soul out of despair. Singing our sadness grants a measure of control in the midst of chaos. If we can put words to our hurt, then we can, in some sense, deal with the harm on our own terms. Singing songs of lamentation turns our mourning into music and creates art out of anguish.

"Hellhound on My Trail" by Robert Johnson	Psalm 143:3–4, a Psalm of David

I got to keep moving, I got to keep moving
Blues falling down like hail, blues falling down like hail
Mmm, blues falling down like hail, blues falling down like hail
And the day keeps on remindin' me, there's a hellhound on my trail
Hellhound on my trail, hellhound on my trail
	The enemy pursues me,
	    he crushes me to the ground;
	he makes me dwell in the darkness
	    like those long dead.
	So my spirit grows faint within me;
	    my heart within me is dismayed.

Lament should also be expressed in prayer. In a worship service, for instance, there should be a crying out to God over the brokenness of the world. Public prayers of lament might include the following:

- a reading of the names of people unjustly killed by law enforcement
- a litany of injustices perpetrated by the local, state, and federal governments we empower
- a confession of the community's failure to love and serve the poor, the prisoner, the widow, and the orphan
- a reading from Scripture that expresses lament (e.g., Ex. 34:8–9; Lam. 1:17–22; Pss. 13; 44; Matt. 23:37–39)

Corporately Confess the Sin of Racism

"Why should I be responsible for the racism of other people?" That is the frequent refrain from racial justice resisters. They may, in principle, accept the idea that a person can be racist and commit racist acts. But they believe that is all just a matter of individual actions. Only the people involved should be responsible for their words and actions. Racial justice resisters will argue that no one can be expected to repent of racist acts they did not personally commit. But their argument fails based on what the Bible teaches about confession.

In 586 BCE, the Babylonians conquered Jerusalem and

sent all the Jewish people into exile. Hundreds of years later, King Cyrus authorized the return of the Jews to Jerusalem and the rebuilding of the temple that had been destroyed. After the temple had been rebuilt, the prophet Ezra prayed and implored Yahweh's forgiveness: "I am too ashamed and disgraced, my God, to lift up my face to you, because our sins are higher than our heads and our guilt has reached to the heavens. From the days of our ancestors until now, our guilt has been great" (Ezra 9:6–7).

As a religious leader of the Jewish people, Ezra understood that he interceded not just for himself but on behalf of an entire people. Though he did not engage personally in the sins of which he asks God for forgiveness, he understood that leaders must take responsibility for those they represent. Ezra references the "days of our ancestors" and likely has in mind the people living at the time when Jerusalem was conquered by the Babylonians. Many of the Jewish people saw their defeat and exile as judgment for rebelling against God. They had failed to worship God alone and had adopted the religious practices of the non-Jewish people around them. Yet all of this happened centuries before Ezra's prophetic leadership of the Jewish people. So why is he confessing to God the sin of a previous generation?

Ezra understood the communal nature of sin and righteousness. Every community sets the boundaries for what beliefs and actions are deemed acceptable. A community can judge racist attitudes and actions acceptable for its members and create the context for individual acts of prejudice. While each person is responsible for his or her own choices, one's moral conscience is formed in relationship with a community of people. This means that all people in that community have a responsibility to examine the boundaries of their bigotry. What has your community tolerated when it comes to racism? What has it permitted as far as prejudice? What has your community determined to be the acceptable pace of change?

All of these questions are matters of corporate responsibility.

When a community fails to confront racism or permits—through action or inaction—racist attitudes and behaviors, it is appropriate to confess and repent of communal failure.

How to Acknowledge Your Church's Racial History

The United States was only on its third president when First Presbyterian Church in Augusta, Georgia, was formed in 1804.[13] The congregation grew and became home to some of the wealthiest and most politically powerful residents in the area. By the time the Civil War broke out in 1861, the church was firmly on the side of the Confederacy.

Leading up to and during the Civil War, all three major denominations—Baptists, Methodists, and Presbyterians—split over the issue of slavery. The Presbyterians split in May of 1861. In August of that year, southern Presbyterians formed a new denomination called the Presbyterian Church of the Confederate States of America (PCCSA). In December, the PCCSA held its first meeting at the First Presbyterian Church of Augusta.[14] The pastor of the church at the time was Rev. Joseph R. Wilson. His son, Woodrow, went on to become President of the United States.

Several months before the first meeting of the PCCSA, Rev. Wilson preached a sermon titled "Mutual Relation of Masters and Slaves as Taught in the Bible." In that message he contended that not only did the Bible sanction slavery, but slavery was a "prime conservator of the civilization of the world, besides being one of the colored man's foremost sources of blessing."[15] Much of this history is only publicly known today because more than 150 years later, George Robertson, the white pastor of First Presbyterian Church, wrote about it and led his congregation in efforts to confess the church's racial sins and move forward in repentance. To do this, Robertson wrote an open letter to his congregation and invited Black preachers and other people of color to preach at the church. He planned conversations, panels, and events to bring information about racism in the community to light. He preached messages about racism and reconciliation that were sure to upset some members of his congregation. Although no such efforts are perfect, acknowledging and confessing racism in the church is a necessary and indispensable step in the journey toward racial justice.

Any church, especially those that have been in existence for a long time, should engage in a process of uncovering and confessing their racial history. This might involve digging into the minutes of elder board meetings and seeing what decisions were made around the subject of race. Some churches excluded Black people from becoming members in their churches until final decades of the twentieth century. Others remained silent while racism ran amok in their communities.

In exploring their racial histories, some churches find cause for gratitude. Second Baptist Church in Little Rock was founded in 1871 and built a church downtown where they still worship to this day. In 1957, Little Rock attracted national attention when Arkansas governor, Orval Faubus, blocked nine Black students, the "Little Rock Nine," from integrating Central High School. In the midst of this crisis, the pastor of Second Baptist, Dale Cowling, was one of a handful of white ministers who publicly supported public school integration. Cowling also served as president of the biracial Ministerial Alliance for the city.[16] Historically white churches will almost always have an uneven record on race at best, but moments of courageous Christianity can be instructive and inspirational in our present-day fight against racism.

Exposing the racial history of a church or other institution may require commissioning a historian to do the research, conduct the interviews, and write the story of the group. It is often best if this person is not a member of the church. You want someone who can tell a respectful but unvarnished story, and when someone has a personal stake in the church, it can be difficult to honestly reveal the community's racist leanings.

Once the data has been gathered, the church leaders should implement a plan to share the information with their congregation members. This should be done with the mindset of shepherds who firmly but carefully prod the sheep on the path they should follow. A church's record on race must be clear, but the information may be painful enough by itself without church leaders unnecessarily adding to the difficulty of the process through brazenness and a lack of pastoral care.

Offering a church's record of racism in a one-minute announcement during a regular service will not do justice to the effort that went into researching and compiling the history. In fact, a cursory address might undermine the entire endeavor by downplaying the significance of the information. Matters this important call for a special meeting dedicated to disseminating the findings and answering initial questions. This meeting should be planned so that the maximum number of people can attend with the date and time made known well in advance. It should be announced during services on Sundays and via other modes of communication. This informational meeting should be followed quickly with a plan of action. What will the church do to proactively move away from its racist past and address any present-day obstacles to racial justice?

Those who preach and teach must also accompany this effort with Sunday School, Bible study, and sermon series to make sure all the constituents have an opportunity to hear the message and process the issues raised from a Christian perspective. These meetings will almost certainly come with difficult questions and powerful emotions from congregation members. Facilitators of these conversations need training—through role-playing, outside consultation, coaching, and more—to deescalate tense situations and answer complex questions with wisdom and empathy.

Finally, a church's record on race should not be hidden from visitors or potential members. It can come as a shock to visitors who, after attending the church, meeting new people, and investing in the life of the congregation, find out that the church they thought they knew has a racist backstory.

To discover this information, often unexpectedly, feels like a betrayal and leaves people wondering why no one told them about it. While it may not be practical to pull aside every visitor to talk about the congregation's racist past, the information should be readily available.

A summary of findings from the study committee could be posted on the "About" page or under the "History" section of a church website. Links to sermon or teaching series on racial reconciliation should be easily discoverable on the website. A list of recommended reading and other resources should also be provided. A link to the church's plan for racial justice should also be publicly posted. Dedicating an entire page or section of the website would even be appropriate.

Acknowledging a church's acts of racist commission and omission can rock a congregation. Members may leave. Donations may diminish. Some may wonder why the church is "bringing up the past." Angry conversations and emails are a near certainty. But only what is revealed can be healed. It does no service to a community to hide its shortcomings. Failures of racial justice must be faced with humility, truth, and courage.

Even though the tendency of officials in any organization is to cover their failures, a church should understand better than any other organization the need for confession. Confession is not just about you; it is about the people you harmed. So even if you did not personally commit the error, you are still responsible for restoring trust and building relationships. If the people who originally practiced racism are not around or refuse to change, then it falls to the present generation to acknowledge those failures and set a new course. The grace of Jesus Christ allows for honesty about one's shortcomings. Redemption is the hope that your past does not have to define your future. It says that even the most notorious acts of discrimination can be transformed into opportunities for healing and change. But a church has not truly reckoned with its racism until it ceases to hide it. Perfection on race is not a requirement for progress, but honesty is.

How a Church Can Reconcile with People It Has Harmed through Racism

The following story stands out for the public nature of the racist incidents and the lengths to which a new generation of white Christians had to go to repair the damage. It also stands out as an example of how attempts at reconciliation do not always have tidy endings. Even decades later, the hurt that Black people and other people of color experienced due to racism lingers, and sometimes so does the anger.

Independent Presbyterian Church in Memphis, Tennessee, formed through a church split in 1965 over whether Black people could be members of the church. A group of interracial students from Rhodes College in Memphis had been conducting peaceful protests at prominent churches in the city. These actions were called "kneel-ins," and interracial groups of students went to a church to see if they would be allowed to enter the building and worship on Sunday. Many churches, such as Second Presbyterian Church, refused to let these groups enter. The white leaders and members charged that the prospective worshipers were only trying to cause a disruption. But Second Presbyterian Church had a long-standing policy of not admitting Black people into the ranks of their church as members.

After an extended and public controversy, the members of Second Presbyterian Church finally voted to change their policy and allow not only for interracial groups to worship on Sunday but to also open up membership to people of color. But not everyone was happy with the decision. A group of about 300 members saw the move toward racial desegregation as a capitulation to "the culture" and a betrayal of the Bible. So they left and formed their own congregation, Independent Presbyterian Church.[17]

Nearly half a century passed before the church's leadership and members began publicly to acknowledge their church's racist and recent founding. In 2009, church leaders formed a committee to study the church's founding and make recommendations to the current members. After months of examination, the committee came up with four recommendations: (1) reveal to the congregation the racist origins of the church, and adopt the denominational stance on race and the gospel, (2) study what the Bible said about individual and corporate repentance, (3) publicly confess and repent of racism, and (4) recommit to serving their local community across racial and ethnic lines.[18]

For its part, Second Presbyterian Church confessed the sin of racial segregation and apologized to the Black protesters who had been turned away during the protests. The pastor at the time, Sandy Willson, undertook a systematic study of the congregation's part in the Memphis kneel-ins in the early 1960s. As historian Stephen R. Haynes relates, when Willson realized "'what the white community had done here on our campus,' he identified and contacted several local African Americans who had been excluded from the church thirty years earlier." At a meeting with church leaders and several of the Black people who had participated in the protest, Willson said church officials were "profoundly sorry and ashamed of what happened . . . [and] intend[ed] to move 180 degrees in the other direction and have been moving there since 1965." The Black participants, understandably and for various reasons, did not accept the apology. The pain and the hurt, as well as the suspicion and the lateness of the white church's apology, made this initial effort at reconciliation too difficult. But the effort to personally reach out to those who had been harmed is a pattern for other churches to follow.

Keep in mind this work is costly and it doesn't always have a storybook ending. The trailblazers of reconciliation and repentance are seldom celebrated for their efforts. For example, Rev. John Hardie was a young minister who became the senior pastor at Independent Presbyterian Church in 2006. One Sunday he preached about interracial marriage and explained how it was not a sin. For most people this should be an obvious and uncontroversial truth, yet several members at IPC expressed strong opposition to the message. Hardie hosted a special meeting shortly thereafter to clarify his comments, but he never relented from calling racial segregation, in society and marriage, a sin. After several unsuccessful attempts to come to an agreement, the leaders of the church accepted Hardie's resignation in 2007.[19] Although Hardie stepped down as pastor from the church, his attempts to move the church forward on the journey of racial justice may have helped clear the path for others to do so in the future.

How to Preach about Racial Reconciliation

Confession requires naming specific sins. In the words of Martin Luther King Jr., spouting "pious irrelevancies and sanctimonious trivialities" will not advance the cause of racial justice.[20] Milquetoast sermons about all people being equal in God's sight and injunctions to treat everyone fairly is like going for a swim and calling it a shower. You get wet, but you don't get clean.

Pastors and other church leaders must know the particular contours of their congregations well enough to identify the racial idols of their people and then tear them down. This cannot be done with hazy pronouncements about equality and racial reconciliation. Grinding racial idols into dust requires specificity in calling out, confessing, and condemning racism in and around a particular community. Merely proclaiming that "racism is wrong" and "we are all equal" in a sermon does not constitute a strong condemnation of racism. Such general statements are too vague to disrupt entrenched racist ideas and practices. Instead, leaders must cite specific beliefs or actions and identify why they are racist.

For example, instead of a general denunciation of racism, talk about theological racism—how Christians may promote the idea, either blatantly or subtly, that European or white American theologians have the "best" or most "trustworthy" theology. Explain how this ethnocentric view of Christianity only puts certain authors on our bookshelves and particular pastors in pulpits while overlooking others. Talk about how white supremacy causes some to perceive theological views coming from people of color not as sources from which we can learn but as inferior and aberrant. Theological racism refuses to see the wisdom and richness of the perspectives of people of color and continue to privilege a narrow set of interpretive tools.

In the book *How to Preach a Dangerous Sermon*, Frank A. Thomas recommends asking five questions in sermon preparation to help spur the moral imagination for justice. These questions apply to more than just preachers. Any person of faith would benefit from querying the text in this manner.

1. Where in this text do we find equality envisioned and represented by physical presence?
2. Where in this text do we notice empathy as a catalyst or bridge to create opportunities to overcome the past and make new decisions for peace and justice?
3. Where do we find wisdom and truth in this ancient text, the wisdom of the ages?
4. Where is the language of poetry and art that lifts and elevates by touching the emotive chords of wonder, hope, and mystery?
5. To what contemporary moral concern would you apply your responses in these four questions?[21]

Not everyone is a preacher, but there are ways for congregation members to ask their leaders for good teaching about racial justice. First, build awareness. Don't assume that pastors have been exposed to the same information as you have, especially when it comes to current events. Philando Castile, a thirty-two-year-old Black man, had been pulled over for a traffic stop in Falcon Heights, Minnesota, on July 6, 2016. His girlfriend, Diamond, and her four-year-old daughter were with him. Castile had calmly informed the police officer, Jeronimo Yanez, that he had a gun in the car, which he was legally licensed to have. Upon hearing there was a weapon in the car, Yanez yelled, "Don't pull it out!" Although Castile had not been reaching for the weapon, Yanez still fired seven times into the car and killed Castile.[22] Prosecutors indicted Yanez for manslaughter and dangerous discharge of a firearm. A year later Yanez was acquitted of all charges. Outrage ensued, and the verdict resulted in more than 1,000 marchers assembling at the Minnesota Capitol in protest. The governor of the state asked, "Would this have happened if the driver were white, if the passengers were white?"[23] In the midst of this reaction, I sent my pastor a text message that said, "Have you thought about saying something [about the verdict and the reaction] in church? Not saying you have to." He had not yet heard of the outcome in the case, but he did make last-minute adjustments to explicitly mention the case and the pain it has caused for many Black people and their allies. I mention this because not everyone will be up-to-date on the latest news. It can be a helpful practice to pass along links to relevant stories and events—don't assume everyone knows what you know.

Most pastors want to minister to the specific needs of their congregants. But pastors are not mind-readers. Parishioners, at times, need to respectfully bring up their concerns about racial justice with the leadership. Depending on your context, an informal conversation or message may not be the best approach. Personally, I have found that writing a letter that outlines my thoughts and requesting a meeting to discuss them usually elicits a response and at least gets me a hearing. There is strength in numbers, so you may want to initiate such actions along with one or two others or a small group to indicate that your concerns are not isolated to a single individual. In any case, you should be able to say that you used the tools at your disposal to make sure racial justice was on the radar for those charged with preaching and teaching in your faith community.

It remains a lamentable truth that there would be no Black church without racism in white churches. Racist ideas and actions have led to segregated pews. This is particularly tragic because the Christian church purports to be an example of a new community gathered in love and fellowship. If the church is to be a beacon of unity, then congregations must accept the task and responsibility of building relationships through confession, repentance, and action.

Chapter 6

HOW TO MAKE FRIENDS

Latecomers looked around in dismay. All the chairs were full, and the only options available were spots leaning against the wall or sitting on the floor. Although the prospect of shifting from one foot to the other or straining to see above or around someone else's head was not appealing, people kept streaming in. They found whatever space they could and waited for the speakers to start.

The gathered group had assembled at a Christian conference for a session entitled "Doing Racial Harmony." Several speakers presented brief talks in the seventy-five-minute time slot. One of the speakers, Black pastor and author Thabiti Anyabwile, presented on "The Dos and Don'ts of Racial Reconciliation." With a smile on his face and a glint in his eyes, Anyabwile jokingly chided the audience for how difficult it had become to make friends across racial and ethnic lines. He reminded them of how easy it used to be when they were kids. "Every one of us at three, or four, or five used to go up to people and say, 'Will you be my friend?' And what happened?" he asked the audience. "We got friends!"[1]

Ask almost anyone for suggestions about what to do about racism, and most people will say we need relationships with people who are different from us. Cross-cultural friendships are one of the most obvious ways to move further down the road of racial justice. But somehow we have complicated what should be a straightforward endeavor. As Anyabwile went on to share, "At some point we stopped doing that because it became weird. I just think we should go back to being weird. And say, 'Hey, listen, I offer you friendship.'"[2]

This chapter explains some ways to build relationships through the offer of friendship to people who are different and how to do so in a healthy manner that honors their story and identity as well as engages in the uncomfortable work of listening to and learning from one another. It is a delicate subject because one can get the impression that all it takes to "fix" racism is having one or two friends of color. While cultivating racially and ethnically diverse relationships is just one aspect of the continuing journey of racial justice, it is an indispensable one.

Essential Understandings

Humility Not Utility

The watchword for interracial friendships is "humility not utility." Every human being holds value in and of themselves simply because we are each an image of the Creator and have intrinsic dignity. A friendship based solely on what the other person can give you and what you can wrest from your connection is not a friendship but a series of exploitative engagements. Ask yourself, "Would I be friends with this person even if the topic of race never came up?"

Listen More Than You Speak

Black people and other people of color have been living and telling their stories for years. At the prospect of having yet another conversation about race, many have honestly exclaimed, "We tired!"

White people need to be sensitive to the fact that although racial conversations may be new to them, they are not new to people of color. This is a reality many racial and ethnic minorities wish they could forget or turn off, but bigotry and prejudice in schools, the workplace, and even the church pose

constant reminders of how they are treated as "other." In the
few moments of casual social interaction they have, racial and
ethnic minorities may not want to talk about what frequently
reminds them of their marginalization.

So, white people, if you ask a Black person or other person
of color to educate you about race, be prepared to hear the
word *no* or *I'm not interested*. This may or may not be about
you personally. It depends on the depth of the relationship, the
level of trust, and the spirit in which you approach a person.
Just remember that Black people and other racial and ethnic
minorities have been through this before, and your newfound
interest in diversity may not be convenient for everyone else.

Race Is Felt

One aspect of humility in cross-cultural relationships is
realizing that this endeavor is not simply a matter of the head
but of the heart. Many people, particularly those in the racial
majority, approach the issue of race and racism from a mainly
cognitive and intellectual perspective. They treat the ongoing
crisis of racism as an abstract, theoretical concept that can
be approached in a detached or somewhat bemused manner.
To some, racism is like debating whether the movie *Die Hard*
is a Christmas movie—an amusing conversation for a while,
but probably not one that matters much in your everyday life.

A humble person recognizes that racism has wrought
untold damage on entire communities. For members of these
groups, talking about racism is visceral and personal. It comes
with smells, tastes, sounds, sights, and physical sensations.
It carries with it injury, pride, and perseverance. Race is felt.
Race is lived.

To approach race as if it only exists in the realm of theory
and thought is to bring an arrogant pride into interactions
that require sober humility. A person of color who reveals the
tenderest parts of their lives likely will not share anything
else with a person who responds with interrogation rather
than empathy. Relationships across racial and ethnic lines

require both head and heart. When in doubt, err on the side of solidarity instead of detached judgment.

As we discuss building diverse relationships, we must realize that meeting people from different racial and ethnic backgrounds will be harder for white people. Our society has been deliberately constructed to keep white people segregated from people of color. It is possible for many white people to live their lives without any meaningful interaction with racial and ethnic minorities. The intentional segregation of the races means many white people will have to go out of their way to meet people from different backgrounds. Adhering to a routine that takes you from majority-white setting to majority-white setting will never put you in a position to interact with people of color in any way beyond the most transactional encounters. What follows are several suggestions for how to create opportunities to break out of your racially homogenous bubble.

Racial Justice Practices

Do Your Homework First

Have you ever tried to talk about race on social media? I don't recommend it. Such attempts devolve into diatribes for people who want to press a particular—usually uniformed and racist—point. Part of the reason bringing up race online is so ineffective is because people have wildly varying degrees of knowledge about race and different people groups, but absolutely anyone can comment.

If one does not have basic understandings of how racism has operated throughout US history, how to define and identify racist acts, or the challenges a specific racial group faces, then it will be difficult to have a conversation. Oftentimes the best way to respond to people who have no clue about race or racism is two simple words: "Google it."

People should take it on themselves to find information about race that is easily searchable online or explicated in detail in dozens of readily available books. Then, even if that person has a different view of the issues, they will at least develop a more informed perspective before engaging in conversation with others.

If this is true online, it is even more true in person-to-person relationships. For people of color, having conversations about race is already exhausting; it is even worse if the other person has no clue about race. If you want to know about someone's racial or ethnic experience, first take the time and make the effort to learn what you can on your own. Basic factual data about immigration patterns, significant historical events, and prominent leaders and voices should be proactively sought out *before* a conversation. The person sitting across from you should not be your sole source of knowledge about race. First, they could be wrong or have idiosyncratic views that are not representative of the majority of people. Second, to be treated as the repository of all things racial is an unfair burden to put on anyone. Third, doing research beforehand demonstrates a minimum level of investment in the relationship as you take ownership of your own ignorance instead of expecting someone else to do it for you. As one tired Black woman put it, "This information is already out there. There are so many resources that exist. If you are serious about hating and ending racism, you will put in the effort to find them. If you love me, do your homework."[3]

Can We Be Friends?

"Hey man, do you drink beer?" I looked at the speaker with a bit of confusion and stammered out an uncertain "Sure."

His name was John, he was white, and we were classmates in a summer seminary course in biblical Greek. "You want to grab a drink sometime after class?" he queried in a thick Alabama drawl. I really wasn't sure if he was asking me out on a date or trying to rope me into a pyramid scheme. Or was this guy a "collector" of cross-cultural friendships that he could put on display for other people in order to demonstrate how not racist he was. I risked the chance that a guy going to school to become a pastor maybe had honorable intentions, and, indeed, he did. He just wanted to be friends.

In our pursuit of friendships with people from a range of racial and ethnic backgrounds, the simplest route is often the most effective. Simply asking someone if they want to talk can be a surprisingly effective practice in helping us get to know people who are different. As human beings, we desire connection and mutuality in relationships. The desire for human connection hardly could have been more apparent than during the novel coronavirus pandemic of 2020. When we could not be present physically with people because of health concerns, many of us realized how much we need relationships and connection. But under ordinary conditions, our society is often so fragmented and individualized that it obscures our foundational desire for meaningful associations with others. It should encourage us to remember that making friends across racial and ethnic lines can be as simple as asking, "Can we talk sometime?"

When seeking to develop meaningful relationships across racial and ethnic lines, start with your existing network of relationships. You already have personal connections with your classmates, coworkers, clients, friends, associates, and acquaintances. Yet how often have you purposely considered the people you know with the goal of intentionally developing cross-cultural understanding? Although we need much more integration across society, when you reconsider your current social networks with the idea of seeking diversity, you may find you know people with an array of experiences, ages, and cultural backgrounds.

With someone you already know, moving from shallow understanding to expansive empathy can be as simple as inviting the person to a meeting and saying, "Tell me about yourself." These early conversations do not have to focus on race or culture. Simply by hearing someone tell their story in their own voice, you will begin to understand more of how they have uniquely experienced the world in terms of their gender, race, ethnicity, culture, language, class, ability, geography, and more. In fact, in some instances it may be more helpful not to ask the person about race at all. They may not be comfortable sharing such a personal and sensitive topic with someone they don't know very well. In other cases, the pain of enduring racism may still be too difficult to share, and a true friend will be sensitive to that.

It is a judgment call, but never overlook the easiest way to learn about someone's racial background. Ask. You could introduce the conversation by saying, "I'm trying to be more intentional about learning how people from different backgrounds see the world in ways I never have because of my race or ethnicity. Would you be willing to share any of your experiences or views regarding race?" You may want to say this when you first invite the person to a conversation. If someone thinks they are just going for a friendly cup of coffee or a low-key lunch and then finds that you want to delve into their racial life story, it can feel like a trap. "I just wanted a salad, fam!" No one likes the feeling of being "ambushed" with a racial conversation.

To racial and ethnic minorities who recoil at the thought of talking to white people about their personal lives and understanding of race, you can and should determine your boundaries. You are not obligated to satisfy anyone's curiosity on demand. You are not the only person of color who can speak to the reality of race and racism. You may, however, consider what telling your story can do for you. Sometimes sharing your story can lead to a rich relationship with someone from a very different social location than you. You might even learn something yourself about race from the other person. These collaborations also demonstrate your dedication to healthy reconciliation and your openness to being surprised by hope. People are eager for your story, and when you are ready, telling your story may even bring unexpected blessings.

Black people and people of color should make the deliberate

effort to learn from one another too. Dialogues between racial and ethnic minorities are vital. Black people need to understand more of the Asian immigrant and Asian American experience. All of us need to hear from Native Americans. People of color have distinct experiences, cultures, and histories. We are all dealing with the impact of white supremacy, but learning from other people who are dealing with racial and ethnic prejudice builds both awareness and alliances.

How to Meet People of Different Racial and Ethnic Backgrounds

Often you will have to go beyond your existing social network to encounter people who are different from you. To do this, you will have to spend time at places in your community that have racial and ethnic diversity. This seems obvious, but it's not a practice many people purposefully employ. If you are physically active, join the local YMCA, YWCA, or community center instead of the private gym or club. Along the same lines, instead of just participating in the church league sports team with people who are very similar to you, join a community sport or activity comprised of people from across your town or city.

Another suggestion for meeting new people is to get your hair cut at a different place. Any Black man will tell you that finding a good barber is like finding the right spouse—once you find that person, you never let them go, and if you ever do leave, it feels like a betrayal. So getting your haircut in a new place is not for everyone. If white people go to a Black barber or hairdresser, they might wonder, *Are they going to know what to do with my hair?* This is a consideration many Black people have had to contend with at some point in their lives. Everyday spots like barbers shops and hair salons are great places to meet people who are different from you and to listen to conversations you may never hear otherwise.

Another option to meet people out of your typical zone of interaction is to participate in free events around your community. You can attend a class on tax preparation or a book reading at your local library. Go to a festival or parade celebrating people from a different racial and ethnic background. The American Indian Center in Chicago, for example, hosts an annual pow wow that is open to the public.

Many colleges and universities have a multicultural week or ethnic-specific groups that host cultural events. Organizers of such events lament that the people who need to attend, those who need to learn more about diverse cultures, seldom do because they think those occasions are "only for minorities." But typically these events are not intended just for the specific racial or ethnic group being celebrated. People of color want white people to understand their cultures and histories. So these events are usually good places not just for learning but also for meeting new people. You will want to check any online materials or contact the organizers just to be sure. It is always easier to ask about the impact of your presence than to get there and realize you may be subverting the purpose of the occasion. If you are in a position to volunteer, these events can be exceptional opportunities for both meeting new people and getting involved in your community. Depending on the volunteer opportunity, you can develop deep relationships with both the people you are serving as well as the people who are volunteering alongside you.

How to Talk to Racial Justice Resisters

Everyone knows someone in real life who is a racial justice resister. These are folks who may claim not to have a "racist bone" in their body, but they remain steadfastly committed to denying the present reality of racism and not doing much to curb it. Some common deflections from racial justice resisters include the following: "The people who keep talking about racism are the real racists," "The problem is that Black people (or another racial or ethnic group) want a handout and won't take advantage of their opportunities," "So-called experts are just liberals with an agenda," and more.

It can often seem like we inhabit different informational ecosystems than racial justice resisters. They simply will not listen to any of the data we can muster to prove our case. Does this mean all is lost? Do we inevitably break relationships with people who outright deny racism and refuse to lift a finger to fight it? In some cases, it may be necessary to end a relationship over racism, but there are still ways to talk to racial justice resisters.

Emma Frances Bloomfield is assistant professor of communication studies at the University of Nevada in Las Vegas. Her research focuses on how scientific misinformation proliferates and how to promote more truthful narratives. The principles she promotes in correcting misconceptions about scientific data can also be applied to correcting misinformation about race and racism. Bloomfield proposes three considerations to help you evaluate how to approach someone who is misinformed on a particular topic.[4]

First, decide whether the topic is worth engaging. How well do you know the other person? Do you have a personal connection as a family member, friend, coworker, or church member? The strength of a preexisting relationship can help you determine in advance your likelihood of persuading someone else of your viewpoint. This question about engaging is especially important in the age of social media. More often than not, engaging with a person you only know online will result in deeper entrenchment and frustration. Your energy is best deployed with someone you know in person rather than a Facebook "friend."

Second, Bloomfield says, "Don't patronize." In a conversation where parties disagree, a condescending tone is easily detectable and kills the opportunity for genuine dialogue. "Instead of treating the conversation as a corrective lecture, treat the other person as an equal partner in the discussion," writes Bloomfield.[5] Christians should readily acknowledge this kind of respect as an aspect of honoring the image of God in others and of loving one's neighbor. It is easier said than done, of course. It takes maturity to treat someone as an equal partner in a dialogue when the other person espouses beliefs and advocates actions that are inimical to your pursuit of racial justice. But respect is a nonnegotiable if you truly want to persuade someone else of your point of view and correct misconceptions.

Third, Bloomfield advises that you offer to "trade information." One way to puncture the misinformation bubble is to offer new sources of information. That is a lot easier to do if you offer to exchange sources instead of just pushing your own. Bloomfield spoke to a climate change skeptic who refused to accept the overwhelming consensus of the scientific community. "Instead of rejecting their resources, I offered to trade with them. For each of their sources I read, they would read one of mine," she wrote.[6]

Besides these strategies, if you are interacting with a Christian, you may want to start with the Bible as a source. Ostensibly, God's Word is a trusted source that would meet with less opposition and skepticism than a book by a professional scholar or some other expert. Walk through the biblical story of race and ethnicity outlined in chapter 2 and discuss specific passages with the person. They will likely not object to the principle of spiritual equality, but when you get to the reality of racism and ask why it seems like so many white people have oppressed people of color, then you can move on to history. Focusing on historical facts that are hard to deny can create cracks in someone's conscience that will allow the truth to pierce through.

The root of resistance to racial justice is the heart. This is not to imply that we should ignore structural and policy issues; it is simply to say that a lack of intellectual knowledge may not be the primary impediment to racial justice. You can stack facts from floor to ceiling, and it may not make a dent in someone's racial recalcitrance. What is necessary is a heart change. This comes through prayer and patience. Never forget that in this war against racial injustice, "Our struggle is not against flesh and blood, but against the rulers, against the authorities, against the powers of this dark world and against the spiritual forces of evil in the heavenly realms." The fight against racism is not against flesh and blood but against "powers and principalities in the heavenly places" (Eph. 6:12).

Find Your Community or Make One

People often ask me how I persevere on the path of racial justice. With all the attacks and accusations, the half-steps and missteps, the slow progress and sometimes regress of the movement—how do we keep going? For me it has been my faith and my community.

For Black people and other people of color, it is imperative that you find a community of like-minded people who can affirm your dignity and encourage you on your journey. For Christians, this community should come through the local church. But such an affirming community is often difficult to find in predominantly white churches and denominations. It is time for many of us to go home to the Black church or other ethnic-specific fellowships. The sad truth is that as long as there is racism in the white church there will always be a need for churches comprised primarily of racial and ethnic minorities. It is not about re-segregating ourselves, it is about gaining the strength to persevere as a person of color in a society enthralled by white supremacy. Ethnic-specific spaces have long provided the strength, expression, awareness, and sensitivity Black people and other people of color need to keep going in the face of racist headwinds.

If you cannot find a local church that embraces your racially and ethnically embodied self, then find one elsewhere. My lifeline in times of racial turmoil has often been text message groups. I can connect with people in different states and time zones to vent, laugh, pray, and reflect. Social media has forums for private groups that can serve a similar function. Perhaps you can find such a group as you participate in activism and service. The point is that no one can fight racism alone. We need a community of people to help us on the way. If such a community is not readily available, then that is not a reason to abandon community but the impetus to creatively pursue it.

The ARC of Racial Justice compels us not to isolate ourselves in homogenous social networks but instead to pursue relationships with people of different racial and ethnic backgrounds. This can be difficult and costly. It can be seen as a capitulation to a shallow form of reconciliation that places too much emphasis on personal relationships and too little emphasis on systemic and institutional racism. But on the journey of racial justice you will need co-workers and compatriots. Not giving up on the power of relationships offers a powerful testimony to the value of fighting racism and the unity such efforts bring.

Chapter 7

HOW TO BUILD DIVERSE COMMUNITIES

The most racially and ethnically inclusive place I've ever worked in was the school I taught at in the Delta. When I say it was inclusive, that does not mean it was perfect. Our leader was a white man from Massachusetts who had learned the importance of diversity, but even he did not always get it right. We sometimes had to point out ways he could treat people of color on staff more equitably. Still, he did his best to listen. Most of the racial conflict we had at the school came not from him but from my fellow coworkers.

We had a diverse staff that included people of African and Asian descent, but most of the team at the school was white. Since over 90 percent of our students and their families were Black, and most of them were low-income, we had to constantly coach and remind one another to treat all of our constituents with dignity. It was that culture of honesty and collaboration, not flawless execution, that made our school feel so different from other schools, churches, and organizations of which I had been a part.

Unfortunately, racially and ethnically inclusive organizations like this one are the exception, not the norm. Many groups do not have diversity on their team in a way that makes minorities feel more welcome. Some leaders do not have the awareness or relationships that would help them understand the perspectives of people of color. Others simply do not consider diversity a priority and cannot see how it would help them do their work any better or differently.

This chapter highlights ways that organizations can become places that practice diversity, equity, and inclusion. While the previous chapter focused on what churches can do to foster diversity, this portion of the book extends the discussion to how any group—religious or not—can pursue racial justice within their own ranks.

Essential Understandings

Diversity, Equity, and Inclusion

Diversity, equity, and inclusion are each distinct principles, and all three are necessary for a healthy organizational culture. If diversity focuses on who is present, equity says who has access to a community's resources and on what terms, and inclusion speaks to the sense of welcome and belonging extended to each person or group. Robert Sellers, chief diversity officer at the University of Michigan, compares diversity, equity, and inclusion (DEI) to a dance. He says, "Diversity is where everyone is invited to the party. Equity means that everyone gets to contribute to the playlist. Inclusion means that everyone has the opportunity to dance."[1]

We must acknowledge that the mere presence of racial variety does not produce racial justice. If an organization desires diversity, that is a laudable goal, but it is only one part of the work of racial justice. Too many people of color have entered majority white spaces only to find that they are valued for their presence but not their perspective.

André Henry is a writer and activist. For a time he worked at a white evangelical publication that posted articles on the web and hosted podcast interviews with Christians to talk about art, culture, and current events. Leaders there hired him to be the managing editor and come up with themes and articles for their blog. According to Henry, when he proposed a series for Black History Month, the senior leader didn't like the idea: "We're going to publish something [about Black history] every day for Black History Month?" When Henry explained that he composed similar schedules for Native American Heritage Month and for the holiday season, his boss shot back, "Oh! So you're just making decisions now?" Deciding content was Henry's job, but he found out in that moment that he did not have the authority to make decisions that he thought he did.[2] This particular workplace had an element of diversity, but not true equity. To build on Sellers' analogy, people of color may be invited to the party, but the music is completely unfamiliar, and no one asks them to dance. In later chapters, we will focus on when it is necessary for Black people and other people of color to form their own organizations, but here I want to emphasize the need to build diversity, equity, and inclusion in an existing—and predominantly white—institution.

Make a Plan, Work the Plan

In addition to addressing diversity, equity, and inclusion, organizations must have a comprehensive plan for creating such a culture. Engaging in half-hearted efforts at diversity can be more devastating than not doing anything at all. Having a superficial plan or forging ahead without the necessary relationships and commitment from relevant constituents can confirm racial stereotypes and create a sense of cynicism about diversity. If it fails due to a lack of conviction and sound planning, people may be tempted to say, "We tried that! All this racial diversity stuff doesn't work. Stop forcing it down our throats."

Every organization should pursue racial and ethnic diversity, but they should do so knowing that a bad plan or a lack of dedication can erect more roadblocks to racial justice than having never engaged in such efforts in the first place. In other words, it takes hard work. But on the other side of that effort is an organization that truly welcomes people from all racial and ethnic backgrounds, makes everyone feel like they have a voice in how business is conducted, and has an opportunity for success. The effort is worth the outcome.

Some may object to an overt focus on race and ethnicity in hiring and building teams within an organization. They will see this as "reverse racism" or perpetuating the problem of racism by constantly focusing on race. "Why not hire based solely on merit and not look at race or ethnicity at all?" they might object. But such assertions are misguided and ahistorical. The history of racial discrimination against Black people and other people of color cannot be corrected by a "colorblind" philosophy. This ignores the systematic ways that people have been excluded on the basis of race or ethnicity and does nothing proactively to offer marginalized people greater access to opportunity. Martin Luther King Jr. said, "A society that has done something special *against* the Negro for hundreds of years must now do something special *for* him, in order to equip him to compete on an equal basis."[3]

In diversifying an organization, it is critical to understand that affirmative action is not "reverse racism." Some might say that paying attention to various kinds of diversity, especially race and ethnicity, makes the same racist mistake in reverse. According to this logic, the only option for an organization looking to become more diverse is to pay less attention to race, not more. In fact, they may even say that race should not be a factor at all in hiring. Only a candidate's qualifications should be taken into account. This sounds like a fair policy until you realize two critical factors.

First, everyone has biases when hiring, often favoring people categorized as white. In a viral video published by Buzzfeed, a man named José Zamora applied to dozens of jobs for several months. No employer ever responded. Then José decided to drop the 's' in his first name and typed "Joe" on all of his applications. The responses came pouring in. "Sometimes I don't even think people know, or are conscious, or aware that they're judging, even if it's by a name," Zamora explains in the video. "But I think we all do it all the time."[4]

Zamora's individual experience has been verified across broader research. In a study published in the *American Economic Review*, two researchers conducted a study on hiring titled, "Are Emily and Greg More Employable than Lakisha and Jamal?" They composed and sent nearly 5,000 fictitious résumés and assigned them either "white-sounding" or "African American-sounding" names, in this case—Emily Walsh and Greg Baker versus Lakisha Washington and Jamal Jones. Controlling for all other factors, the résumés with white-sounding names got 50 percent more call backs than those with African American sounding names.[5] Perhaps none of the hiring managers consciously attempted to exclude applicants based on something as superficial as how their name sounds, but this illustrates the power of bias in a culture crafted along racial lines. Since implicit racial biases can exert such a powerful force, proactive measures to ensure racial and ethnic diversity are necessary and must be implemented.

Second, if a racial or ethnic group has been systematically and intentionally *excluded*, then when it comes time to build more diversity, that racial group must be systematically and intentionally *included* as well. A variety of factors—from the quality of education available in particular communities, to housing patterns, to access to professional and social networks—have been historically crafted to include or exclude certain groups based on race. The church, unfortunately, is a prime example of this trend.

As I mentioned earlier, Presbyterians, Baptists, and Methodists all split in the period leading up to the Civil War because of disputes over whether one could hold slaves and still be a Christian in good standing. During the late nineteenth and early twentieth centuries, many predominantly white churches excluded Black people from membership and ordination. Prominent Christian leaders such as G. T. Gillespie of Belhaven College (now university) and Bob Jones, founder of Bob Jones University, actively promoted racial segregation and excluded people of color from their colleges. The Southern Baptist Theological Seminary, founded in 1859, took nearly a century to begin moving toward racial desegregation in the 1940s and 1950s and remained skeptical of the Civil Rights movement thereafter.[6] Other places of higher education such as the University of Mississippi did not admit Black students until 1962, and even this small gesture was accompanied by rioting white people and two deaths.

In the face of outright historic discrimination, simply removing the legal barriers to desegregation does not counteract the effect of decades of discrimination. The solution to imbalanced hiring practices that have historically favored white people is not the adoption of a "race-blind" process. As one historian put it, "race-blind policies in a race-conscious society can make access by minorities too difficult."[7] By contrast, proactive measures, or affirmative actions, are necessary to level the uneven playing field. Intentional practices are needed that focus on the racial and ethnic groups these institutions once rejected. This means that any organization that wants to increase racial and ethnic diversity must intentionally seek it and make that desire known.

Many white leaders of organizations may hesitate to explicitly state their desire to hire racial or ethnic minorities. They do not want to be accused of discriminating against another racial demographic or of favoring one group over another. This is an understandable but misguided sentiment. If anyone levels an accusation of favoritism against you, you can point out that, historically, policies and practices have favored white people over people of color. Intentionally seeking out racial and ethnic diversity is not an attempt to exclude white people but to include people who have been underrepresented because of racist beliefs and biases.

Racial Justice Practices

How to Do a Group Study on Race

Though it may initially seem like an odd place to start, forming a book study or Bible study group focused on racial justice is actually one of the best ways to both increase awareness and build relationships. The basic premise of these groups is that you gather people, usually diverse in their racial and ethnic backgrounds, around a piece of content and over the course of several weeks or months journey together into deeper levels of cross-cultural understanding. In forming these groups, I've found there are some key habits to keep in mind.

First, cultivate diversity to the extent possible. Every group, especially those focused on learning about race and ethnicity, benefits from diverse perspectives on the topic. Although it may feel uncomfortable, it is alright to intentionally seek racial diversity in a group. One way to do this is to specifically invite people who represent a range of cultures. Another way to foster diversity in a small group is to gather a list of all interested parties and divide them up based on what you know about their cultural locations.

As you begin your meetings, start with stories. In many groups, members will not know each other at all or only be familiar on a superficial level. It is also hard to dive right into a controversial subject without having built trust first. Invite participants to talk about themselves. What are their hopes for the group? Why did they join? How did they first become interested in the topic of racial justice? Sharing stories humanizes each person and helps group members see each other as individuals with unique histories and contributions. This will be an asset as the conversation moves more explicitly to the subject of race and differences of opinion become more apparent.

Build Diversity into the DNA of Your Organization

At the 2015 General Assembly for the Presbyterian Church in America (PCA), Rev. Jim Baird, a white man who had pastored the historic First Presbyterian Church of Jackson, Mississippi, rose to the microphone in front of hundreds of his fellow ministers. They were debating whether to adopt the "Personal Resolution on Civil Rights Remembrance" that would acknowledge the denomination's inaction and complicity with racism during the 1950s and 1960s. Baird rose in support of adopting the resolution and gave a rationale for his stance. "I confess, that in 1973, the only thing I understood was that we were starting a new denomination, which we did. And I confess that I did not raise a finger for civil rights." He went on to say, "Were we racists? No. But we did not do anything to help our black brethren."[8]

Whatever the personal convictions of the twelve men credited with formally establishing the denomination, they did not take proactive steps to form a racially and ethnically inclusive denomination. Add to this the overt forms of racism that still persisted among some leaders, and the result is predictable.[9] Nearly half a century later, the PCA maintains an overwhelmingly white cadre of ordained ministers. Out of nearly 5,000 men ordained to teach and preach, Black men comprise just over 1 percent.[10]

Imagine if the PCA had started with the express intention of being racially and ethnically diverse? What if your organization had started with broad representation among its founders and a plan for making equity and inclusivity a priority? The trajectory for many organizations might be drastically different today had they started with diversity as a priority. Too many organizations and their leaders have seen racial and ethnic diversity as a "nice to have" or an optional add-on, like an elective class in high school or college. Yet in reality diversity is part of the required curriculum for healthy and inclusive organizations and no education is complete without it. The earlier an organization realizes this, the easier it is to cultivate diversity.

Many of the following suggestions focus on organizations that have only recently committed to fostering a racially and ethnically diverse and inclusive environment. These organizations still have to do the difficult and lengthy work of dismantling existing systems as they rebuild new ones that can accommodate people from various backgrounds. Much of this work can be avoided in new organizations by simply making racial and ethnic diversity a core value from the beginning and crafting an organization's ethos and practices accordingly. It is easier to end up with diversity if it is part of your organization from the start.

Build a Case for "Why"

According to a Pew Research survey, about 75 percent of Americans say that "to promote racial and ethnic diversity in their workplace" is either "somewhat" or "very important." That's a good sign. It means that most people welcome some racial and ethnic diversity at their jobs. But racial and ethnic minorities, especially Black people, are more likely to place a premium on diversity. Sixty-seven percent of Black respondents and 52 percent of Hispanic respondents indicated that promoting diversity in the workplace was very important, as compared to 43 percent of white respondents.[11] In practice, this means that even if a person values racial and ethnic diversity in the workplace, different groups will be more or less enthusiastic about efforts to attain that diversity.

Since opinions about the relative importance of such efforts can differ among groups, predominantly white institutions (PWIs) should begin the process of increasing racial diversity, equity, and inclusion by building a case for "why." Don't assume everyone values racial diversity or that they are willing to take the necessary actions to achieve it. Many who resist racial justice efforts think diversity is about political correctness or pragmatic concerns about the changing complexion of the nation. If that is the case, then diversity initiatives will face vocal opposition or, at best, begrudging acceptance. Racial justice efforts will inevitably stall without the commitment of all parties involved, especially the leadership.

Building a case for "why" explains that diversity, far from being a box to check or just another program to execute, actually enhances the effectiveness of the organization.

Numerous studies indicate that diversity on a team leads to better decision-making because members can account for different perspectives on an issue. Diversity can help with hiring too. According to projections, 75 percent of the workforce will be occupied by members of the millennial generation by 2025. Of this group, 47 percent actively seek diversity in the workplace.[12]

To build a case for why, it often helps to start on an individual basis. A significant and controversial initiative cannot simply be announced in an organization-wide message. You have to build consensus through one-on-one or small group meetings. Approaching large groups of people in smaller, more personal settings before the big meeting allows you to answer objections and concerns at-length and with more specificity. It also defuses the defensiveness some people may display because they have been introduced to an idea and have had time to contemplate it. Once you have communicated with key constituents, then you can begin communicating more broadly.

You can also build a case for why by referencing the organization's existing documents or principles. Instead of starting with no material, go back and explore the mission and vision statement. Look at the strategic plan or other relevant documents and meetings. You may find that the organization has already made a written commitment to racial justice, and the initiatives you want to propose simply put those words into action.

Building the "why" is a critical step in making an organization more diverse because it cultivates personal investment from the people who have responsibility for leadership and change. Plowing ahead without offering a tailored case for why diversity is a value and should be pursued may end up demolishing more than can ever be constructed.

Assemble the Team

Harvesting a crop is the result of extensive labor even before a seed hits the ground. The land has to be cleared and fertilized. An adequate water source must be available. Then the ground is tilled, and seeds are planted. Eventually, after weeks of waiting, the first sprouts begin to break the surface. The work is still not done though. The plants must be watered and protected from grazing animals, pests, severe weather, and weeds. Then, finally, after constant care and attention you can reap the harvest.

It's the same with developing ethnic and racial diversity in an organization. In-depth internal work must be done before the first job posting goes out or the first statement on diversity is written and published. One of the first steps to doing this internal work entails gathering a team that will facilitate but not be solely responsible for the work of increasing diversity. This could be an ad hoc group or a standing committee on diversity. Ideally, this team reflects the diversity to which the organization aspires and should be made up of people from a variety of racial and ethnic backgrounds.

A major function of this team should be to diagnose the specific problems and issues that the organization faces in terms of diversity. An easy mistake to make is to take action without fully understanding the problem first. This group should engage in several practices to enhance their effectiveness. Reading a book or engaging some other form of multimedia content should be one of the first steps. In addition, this group can be in charge of delving into the history of the organization. They could research the first person of color hired by the company and possibly invite that person or group to address the organization. They might conduct interviews with focus groups of others in the organization. Before undertaking organization-wide change, it may be wise to launch and oversee a pilot program aimed at increasing cultural awareness and diversity, equity, and inclusion.

Adopt a Statement on Racial Justice

Every organization that is committed to racial justice should have a written statement that expresses their views.

This statement should be shared internally with employees and other stakeholders. It should also be publicly available in annual reports and on websites. The statement functions as an explicit articulation of what an organization values in terms of racial justice and unfolds the rationale for their beliefs on this issue.

For racial and ethnic minorities, seeing such a statement communicates at least two messages. First, a statement on diversity, equity, and inclusion indicates that the organization's leadership has thought through issues related to race. Second, it provides an official policy to appeal to if an incident occurs or if a new or existing practice contradicts the organization's stated commitment to racial justice.

The problem with a statement on racial justice is that it can become a zombie document. It lives on a website or in a report somewhere, but in practice it is dead. A zombie document on racial justice has just enough life to give the appearance of vitality, but it provides none of the growth or change that would indicate viability. A document on racial justice is not in itself racial justice. It is a written expression of a desire, not the fulfillment of that desire.

Actions must back up the words on the page. But just because a statement is not sufficient to encompass racial justice efforts, that does not mean it is unnecessary. A statement on racial justice is valuable not simply for the document itself but also for the process of creating it. The readings, the meetings, the conversations, the consultations, the debates—all of these elements build awareness, develop relationships, and move further toward actual commitment to equity. Like the journey toward racial justice, crafting a statement on racial justice is about the process, not just the outcome.

Require Applicants to Submit a Statement on Racial Justice

It is not enough simply to hire for diversity; you have to know what a person believes about race and ethnicity and about their commitment to equity and inclusion. When hiring new people, have potential candidates write or make a verbal explanation about their commitment to racial justice. No single conversation—for example, in an interview—can tell you everything you need to know, but having a person explain their views can help you evaluate whether a candidate's perspectives on the topic align with the organization's direction.

These statements help you assess a person's "cultural intelligence." Cultural intelligence indicates a person's capacity to be aware of and responsive to the various backgrounds of the people with whom they interact. In a nation with a dizzying amount of diversity—from languages, to nations of origin, to religion, and more—the ability to relate to people vastly different from oneself is essential. A statement on racial justice or about diversity, equity, and inclusion can serve as an introduction to a person's cultural intelligence.

In the statement, look for a track record of prioritizing racial justice. Anyone can string together some words that sound good on paper, but ask yourself what they have actually done to mentor, train, invest in, and support racial and ethnic minorities. You also need to evaluate whether this person will enhance your present strategies. See if they have a plan for how they can contribute to the organization's goals for racial justice and whether their approach fits yours.

To assess the views of a potential team member, you can ask questions such as the following: What is racial justice? Describe how you have demonstrated a commitment to racial justice. What is the current state of racial justice in _____ (use whatever field you're in: church, higher education, housing, etc.)? These statements from prospective candidates will not give you all the relevant information about a person's racial beliefs, but they will provide an important data point for your evaluation.

Hire in Clusters

Hiring more people of color in order to diversify an organization may seem like a good idea at first, but in practice, it can create a scenario for disappointment and even trauma. Any predominantly white institution—colleges and universities, corporations, churches, and more—that wants to move toward racial justice will at some point say, "We need to hire more people of color." It makes sense. If you want to demonstrate a commitment to racial justice, then your team will have to reflect more racial and ethnic diversity.

The typical route to diversifying your staff is to go on a search for one person to fill one position. But try to understand this from the perspective of a racial or ethnic minority. You ask yourself questions such as, "Do I want to do this job on top of being the first person of color there? Is this situation going to be healthy not only for me but for my family too? Do the people in this organization really want to change in substantial ways, or will I be used as a token of diversity?"

In addition, hiring one person to represent all diversity at the organization risks shuffling the responsibility for racial responsiveness onto the shoulders of just one person. If the rest of the team believes, in practice if not in word, that the lone Black person or Asian American should handle all of the "race issues," then comprehensive organizational change is impossible. Everyone on the team has to have a stake in becoming a more racially just organization, and they cannot abandon their own role in creating change.

Since hiring for racial and ethnic diversity is so fraught, should an organization even attempt to do so? Of course! The solution is not to hire fewer people of color but to hire more at the same time. In other words, hire in clusters. Cluster hiring means hiring several people at once who have overlapping interests and expertise in various departments and roles in an organization. Cluster hiring has been especially utilized in the field of higher education to create diversity in terms of both race and ethnicity as well as fields and research areas. At Emory University, faculty and staff hired in clusters to dramatically change the racial and ethnic makeup of some departments. Carla Freeman, senior associate dean of faculty at Emory University's College of Arts and Sciences, tells the story: "In the three years leading up to our cluster-hire experiment—between 2014 and 2017—Emory hired a total of 65 tenure-track faculty members, only 15 percent of whom were from underrepresented groups." Then they made a shift to hiring in clusters. "Between 2017 and 2019, after adding cluster hiring to our other efforts, we've recruited 80 new tenure-track faculty members, 51 percent of them (or 41 hires) from underrepresented groups."[13]

Cluster hiring requires a vast amount of resources, especially money. Organizations can seldom hire for more than one position at a time, but racial justice requires resources. Reevaluating budget priorities is unavoidable if significant change is to occur. Even more difficult than assembling the financial resources is mustering the willpower from a significant number of stakeholders to pursue cluster hiring and diversity in the first place.

In addition to hiring for diversity, it will be necessary to cultivate a diverse hiring team. A racially homogenous team can replicate biases and blind spots even when they are actively recruiting for diversity. Having racial and ethnic diversity in the hiring process may require revising the process altogether to allow for members of different departments and ranks to participate. It may also be advisable to work with consultants who can help your organization sort through applicants with an eye toward racial and ethnic diversity and cultural competence.

The investment in cluster hiring is worth it. While not without opposition and shortcomings, this practice has increased faculty retention in higher education institutions and has created a more inclusive climate for students. The same can be true of any organization in any field of work. Instead of heaping the burden of overcoming racial injustice on the back of a single person designated as the "diversity hire," a cluster of people who come in with the same mindset can help shift an organization's beliefs and practices across constituencies and have a better chance at surviving a predominantly white institution as well.

How to Pursue Diversity Even If Your Organization Remains Homogenous

It's a hard reality to face, but sometimes no amount of zeal, study, or sincerity will result in significant racial or ethnic diversity in your organization or congregation. Sometimes, it is simply a matter of demographics. States such as Vermont, Maine, and Iowa all have populations that are over 90 percent white. What is true of states can also be true of organizations. Can such racially homogenous places meaningfully pursue diversity?

If your organization is located in a place that does not have much racial diversity, you still have a stake in racial justice. First, you need to teach the principles of diversity, equity, and inclusion because the people there now may one day move on to someplace different. You should equip your people for the day when they may enter a new space and encounter more racial and ethnic diversity. Second, most homogenous organizations are only mostly homogenous, that is, there are still some Black people and other people of color present, even if only in small numbers. For their sake, you must take on racial justice to ensure a healthy environment. Third, we should remember there are all kinds of diversity beyond race or ethnicity. Every organization should cultivate geographic, gender, and class diversity. None of these necessarily have to do with race or ethnicity, but they can all lend indispensable perspectives from a variety of social and cultural locations. Finally, every organization can support other organizations that have more racial and ethnic diversity. Some of these ways will be outlined in later chapters. For now, it is necessary simply to commit to making every effort to diversify your organization, even if that diversity feels out of reach.

Organize Yourselves

Black people and other people of color often find themselves in predominantly white settings. Whether it is school, church, or the workplace, we are often in the position of being a minority within a majority-white organization. Sometimes we can leave; other times, for various reasons, we must stay. If that is the case, then it is best to organize with like-minded individuals for change.

When it comes to fighting racism, there is strength in numbers. A lone voice is easy to silence or ignore, but a chorus of voices is easier to hear. First, look at the organization's grievance policy—it may not focus explicitly on incidents of racism, but it can provide valuable information about how to lodge a complaint. You want to make sure no one can discredit your claims based on a procedural issue. Second, gather a group of others who are willing to share any experiences of racial or ethnic discrimination along with yours. If you are experiencing a hostile work environment because of racism, it is likely that others have as well. Find them and ask if they would be willing to talk about their experiences in a written letter, email, or a small group meeting with management. Third, have a specific list of outcomes and changes you want to see. The greater the specificity of your demands, the more likely they will be discussed and perhaps implemented. Finally, if you have followed all the necessary procedures, be prepared to take your requests to the Board of Directors or a similar body. You may even need to go public in order to increase the urgency for change. If all else fails, it may be time to move on.

When to Leave an Organization over Racism

Chanequa Walker-Barnes, the theologian I mentioned in chapter 5, left her staff position at a predominantly white church in the months following the 2016 presidential election. In an article for the *New York Times* she is quoted as saying, "We were willing to give up our preferred worship style for the chance to really try to live this vision of beloved community with a diverse group of people. . . . That didn't work."[14] The divide between how white and Black Christians viewed issues like national politics had become too great.

Black pastor Lawrence Ware renounced his ordination in the Southern Baptist Convention in 2017. "My reasoning is simple," he wrote in an op-ed. "As a black scholar of race and a minister who is committed to social justice, I can no longer be part of an organization that is complicit in the disturbing rise of the so-called alt-right, whose members support the abhorrent policies of Donald Trump and whose troubling racial history and current actions reveal a deep commitment to white supremacy."[15]

I, too, felt compelled to leave my predominantly white southern Presbyterian denomination and a staff position I held at the seminary I attended. The decision was not easy. It cost me relationships and created immense emotional strain. But sometimes, for Black people and other people of color, one must move on from an organization that does damage to your emotional and spiritual health.

How do you know when it's time to leave? There is no perfect formula, but here are some considerations:

- Are you suffering so much emotional and mental trauma that you are having health problems?
- Have your repeated attempts to bring up issues of racial equity and diversity not only met with a lack of action but with anger and aggressiveness?
- Have your attempts to raise concerns using the approved mechanisms for filing grievances failed?
- Has the organization ignored its stated plan for diversity, equity, and inclusion?
- Have you been denied institutional authority to implement changes?
- Have other racial and ethnic minorities had similar experiences?

If any of the above are true, then you may need to give serious consideration to leaving the organization. I made the step to separate from some of the predominantly white organizations with which I was affiliated when I saw that people I thought I could trust remained silent in the face of the racism I experienced. After the 2016 presidential election, other Christians came after me through trolling on social media, angry emails, and slander in blog posts and online articles because I did not support Donald Trump. I expected these overt forms of opposition. What I was less prepared for was the lack of public support from people I considered friends. People with whom I worked or attended church privately affirmed me, but they were silent amid the public attacks I endured. It is not true racial solidarity if your support ends the moment you must publicly align with someone who has been publicly maligned.

Unfortunately, not every organization or their leaders are ready or willing to take the steps necessary to foster diversity, equity, and inclusion. In the meantime, racial and ethnic minorities suffer the worst effects of these shortcomings. You do not have to stay in such environments forever. You may have been there for a phase of your life. You may have met some incredible people. But there is a season for everything, and moving on could be a sign of maturity and growth.

The ARC of Racial Justice means that organizations must commit energy and resources to building healthy relationships. The effort is not a one-time decision but an ongoing commitment to listen and respond to the unique needs of different groups. Organizations that fail to do this not only limit their ability to fulfill their mission, but they leave a trail of hurt and harm in their wake. Alternatively, your organization could, with time and consistent effort, become a healthy environment for all different kinds of people and an example for others to follow.

PART 3

COMMITMENT

Chapter 8

HOW TO WORK FOR RACIAL JUSTICE

Three hundred and eighty-one. That's how many days the Montgomery Bus Boycott lasted. Sparked by lifelong activist and justice-seeker Rosa Parks, fueled by Black women who organized car pools, printed flyers, and walked to and from work, and with Martin Luther King Jr. as the spokesperson of the Montgomery Improvement Association (MIA), Black people brought the city to a standstill and forced white civic and business leaders to change their segregationist policies.

Just a few weeks before the formal end of the boycott, King gave the opening speech at MIA's Institute on Nonviolence and Social Change, a weeklong series of lectures and workshops for activists. The theme that year was "Freedom and Justice through Love," and in that address, King mentioned the concept of the "beloved community."[1] He said, "It is true that as we struggle for freedom in America we will have to boycott at times. But we must remember as we boycott that a boycott is not an end within itself." Rather, he explained, "the end is reconciliation; the end is redemption; the end is the creation of the beloved community."[2]

The concept of the beloved community can sound like a utopian dream rooted in an ineffectual idealism that stands powerless against racial injustice, but that is not how King and others thought of the beloved community. They understood love as the fire that fueled their adamant demand for change. Love requires the use of power. In his roadmap to racial justice *Where Do We Go from Here*, King wrote, "Power, properly understood, is the ability to achieve purpose. It is the strength required to bring about social, political or economic changes." He went on to explain, "Power at its best is love implementing the demands of justice. Justice at its best is love correcting everything that stands against love."[3] Love is not a mere feeling of affection. In the beloved community, love is an action that uses the levers of power to bring about justice.

Unfortunately, many white Christians have become de facto defenders of an unjust status quo by maintaining that Christians should not get involved in matters of public justice. Their reasoning is multifaceted. Some contend that matters of justice are too "political." The church should stand above and apart from politics so it can effectively preach salvation through Jesus Christ. Others avoid issues of justice because they see in modern descriptions of the problem a pernicious co-optation of the faith by secular philosophies such as Marxism and critical race theory. Still others fail to see any issues in systemic terms and think that society's inequalities stem only from individual choices and effort apart from broader structures.

What is missing from these criticisms is the Christian concept of love. Love for neighbor requires critiquing and dismantling unjust systems of racial oppression. It is one matter to acknowledge that all people are made equal and have inherent dignity in their very being. It is another matter to identify the ways the image of God is defaced in groups of people through systems and policies and to work against those injustices. The emphasis here is on life together in a nation under laws and policies. If Christians claim to be concerned for their neighbors, then they must also be concerned about the structures and systems that enable or inhibit their neighbors' flourishing. As pastor Mika Edmondson wrote, "You cannot love your neighbor while supporting or accepting systems that crush, exploit, and dehumanize them."[4]

The present chapter opens the "commitment" section of

the ARC of Racial Justice. In chapter 2, I explained a biblical vision for racial and ethnic equality based on the concept of the image of God. Now I want to take that further, building on the concept of the dignity of individuals and extending it to matters of public justice rooted in love of neighbor. This chapter emphasizes how churches and faith communities can commit to changing racist policies. Subsequent chapters will broaden the focus to entities of all kinds.

Essential Understandings

Love for God and Neighbor

Love is the fiery heart beating at the center of the urgent call for justice in our world. Love is the energizing force of justice that insists on fairness and equity for all. Love is the motivating factor that demolishes any paternalistic attitudes and builds a posture of humble service. Without love there can be no justice.

Throughout Jesus' public ministry, the scribes and Pharisees, who were Jewish teachers of the law and religious leaders of the day, attempted to discredit him by asking questions designed to entrap him. After foiling a series of such questions, one of the Jewish leaders was impressed with Jesus' answers. So he asked Jesus a question that religious scholars had been debating for years: "Of all the commandments, which is the most important?" (Mark 12:28).

Jesus summarized the most important commands of the Christian faith with a simple remark that most people who grew up in the church can recall from memory: "'Love the Lord your God with all your heart and with all your soul and with all your mind and with all your strength.' The second is this: 'Love your neighbor as yourself.' There is no commandment greater than these" (Mark 12:30–31). Jesus encapsulated the core of Christianity as love for God and love for neighbor. This love animates the call for racial justice.

Notice that Jesus juxtaposes love for God with love for neighbor. The greatest command is to love God with your entire being: heart, soul, mind, and strength. No part of us should be withheld from devotion to God. This is true love for God. But how do we and others know that we love God with our whole selves? Love of God is demonstrated through love of others. While Jesus distinguishes between loving God and loving others, he does not separate the two. It is impossible to love God and hate those whom God has created in God's own image. The apostle John put it this way: "Anyone who loves God must also love their brother and sister" (1 John 4:21). Or as Fannie Lou Hamer put it, "Ain't no such thing as I can hate anyone and hope to see the face of God."[5]

We should also note that when Jesus says to love God and love your neighbor, he is not giving a new interpretation of the Law. The first part of his answer comes from Deuteronomy 6:4–5, which is part of the *shema*, a prayer that observant Jews recited twice daily to remind them of the exclusivity of God and their wholehearted allegiance to God. The book of Leviticus codifies Jewish ceremonial law. It describes laws about bodily discharges, what to do with pieces of an animal killed in sacrifice, which grains to bring for offering, and more. It can be grisly, tedious reading. Yet this book also includes Leviticus 19:18, which says, "Do not seek revenge or bear a grudge against anyone among your people, but love your neighbor as yourself. I am the LORD." Love of God and love of neighbor have been a foundation of Judeo-Christian belief for centuries.

The apostle Paul builds on the necessity of love in 1 Corinthians 13:

> If I speak in the tongues of men or of angels, but do not have love, I am only a resounding gong or a clanging cymbal. If I have the gift of prophecy and can fathom all mysteries and all knowledge, and if I have a faith that can move mountains, but do not have love, I am nothing. If I give all I possess to the poor and give over my body

to hardship that I may boast, but do not have love, I gain nothing. (1 Cor. 13:1–3)

The impetus for public justice in the Christian life comes from the ethical demands of love. The most eloquent words and greatest talents of preaching or teaching about justice amount to a discordant cacophony if those utterances are not undergirded by love. The deepest knowledge of theology, politics, history, and science mean nothing if love is not the ligament binding that information together. Even the most admirable sacrifices, like giving away all your money to the poor or spending your life suffering for the sake of others, are only a form of pseudo-saviorism if those efforts are not infused with love. You cannot pursue justice without love.

Fighting Racism Is Bearing Witness to Christ

Love for God and love for neighbor mean that preaching the gospel and working for racial justice are not at odds; each one needs the other. Some Christians have attempted to insert a wedge between the task of evangelism—proclaiming the good news about Jesus Christ and the salvation he offers—and the task of racial justice. This is a false dichotomy.

Christ called his followers to bear witness about him throughout the world (Acts 1:8). This witness necessarily includes not only the verbal announcement to "repent and believe" but also the imitation of Christ's concern for the marginalized and oppressed. In Matthew 25, Jesus so closely identifies with those who experience hardship that he says to serve them is to serve him. When we feed the hungry, show hospitality to the stranger, clothe the naked, look after the sick, and visit the imprisoned, we have done the same to Christ. He says, "Truly I tell you, whatever you did for one of the least of these brothers and sisters of mine, you did for me" (Matt. 25:40). To care for those who endure injustice, including racism, is to bear witness to Christ himself and to declare his goodness in word and deed.

This chapter focuses on the actions that congregations can take in order to fight for racial justice. Many of these practices can be undertaken as an individual, or they can be done as a church or denomination. These practices may not, on the surface, appear to deal directly with race, but broader issues of justice are nearly always connected to racial discrimination. So while planning a voter registration drive or adopting a public school may not explicitly deal with race, since so many injustices fall disproportionately on racial and ethnic minorities, these can still be considered racial justice practices.

Racial Justice Practices

Steward Your Budget for Justice

Jill McCrory faithfully pastored her church, Twinbrook Baptist, for several years, but the small congregation never grew beyond a few dozen people. They came to the difficult decision to close the church doors and sell the property, but afterward they did something unusual with the money. They took the one million dollars they got from the sale and gave it to thirty-five religious organizations and nonprofits. They also ensured that the Hispanic congregation that had been renting their building could buy it for below-market price. When asked why her church members chose to give away the money, McCrory replied, "Rather than serve ourselves and spend down all the assets and all the budget and then just have this building . . . we felt that the appropriate thing to do was to close and sell the building and then gift out those assets."[6]

While most churches may not be selling their buildings or have seven-figure dollar amounts to spend, the example of Twinbrook Baptist Church still stands as a model for us all. Perhaps instead of doing a capital campaign to raise funds for a new building, your church might use that money to help local nonprofits and other churches. Consider taking up a special collection to support another church. Host a community organization or congregation in your facility free of charge. Spend less on internal programs and allocate that money for community organizations.

Many racial justice practices include a redistribution of money because racism has always been closely related to economic exploitation and greed. The point of this practice is not to ascribe a monetary value to racism or racial justice but to acknowledge and address the clear financial dimensions of discrimination.

Host a Candidate Forum

Churches on the margins tend to have an easier time integrating faith and justice because they have endured the pernicious effects of injustice firsthand. In the United States, the Black church has developed a long and potent tradition of working for justice in the name of the Savior they claim. Historically, Black Christians have not hesitated to get involved in politics because policies enacted by legislators have often been closely tied to their health and safety. Charles H. Pearce (1817–1887) was a Black minister who helped start the first African Methodist Episcopal Church in Florida in the Reconstruction era immediately following the Civil War. Pearce said, "A man in this state cannot do his whole duty as a minister except if he but looks out for the political interests of his people."[7] Much of the Black church tradition distinguishes between the mission of the church and the workings of political bodies, but they have always seen the interrelatedness of the two in the cause of justice.

The tradition of relating politics and faith continues to the present-day. In 2020, Progressive Baptist Church, a prominent church in Chicago pastored by Charlie Dates, hosted a candidate forum between two candidates for state's attorney. While some may object to a church serving as a forum for political discussions, churches like Progressive Baptist seek to foster respectful dialogue and responsible information sharing. While carefully avoiding endorsing particular individuals or parties, the church was able to participate in the political process and perhaps even elevate it for a time. The debate moderator remarked, "They're doing pretty good, right? . . . They're sticking on time, giving thoughtful answers." To which one of the candidates quipped. "We're in a church. We're following rules."[8]

A church interested in hosting a candidate forum should extend the invitation to all candidates. It is up to each candidate and their campaign to decide whether they can or want to attend, but every candidate should have the option. In preparation for the forum, the church leaders should educate the congregation about why and under what circumstances it is permissible for a church to get involved in politics. The purpose of the forum is to give candidates a platform to express their visions for leadership. It is not to endorse a particular candidate or party. In addition, candidate forums should be made open to the public when appropriate. Churches have been and often still are central meeting places for communities, and inviting the public to attend a candidate forum communicates that the church and Christians are interested in more than just spiritual salvation but care also for the entire well-being of the neighborhood, city, state, and nation.

Black churches and congregations comprised of other marginalized groups have valuable lessons to teach about how to attend to the political concerns of their people without the church necessarily devolving into a tool of particular politicians or parties. Informing people of political issues and opening up church facilities to host forums on politics does not forfeit the mission of the church; it is an expression of that mission.

Host a Voter Registration Drive

Voting is one of the most fundamental rights of an individual in a democracy. This is not a partisan issue where one has to support the Republican Party or the Democratic Party. It is an issue of having access to voice one's priorities in a democracy. Churches can promote voting rights broadly without the pressure to promote a certain policy or candidate.

Each state has different requirements for voter registration, so be sure to check with your state's Secretary of State office for the most up-to-date information. You can also learn some of the basics from the US Election Assistance Commission, an independent bipartisan commission that provides support for election officials.[9]

Hosting a voter registration drive at your church will involve several elements. Determine when the deadline for voter registration is for your state, and procure the relevant forms needed to register people. Announce when and where the drive will take place. Gather volunteers to help register people to vote. You might want to host an informational meeting for volunteers so they can answer questions and ensure that registrants complete the process correctly. Be sure to announce and publicize the date and hours of the drive.

In order to maintain the tax-exempt status most churches enjoy, the Internal Revenue Service (IRS) has clear guidelines about how churches can and cannot be involved politically. The general rule is that churches cannot endorse particular candidates, parties, or platforms, and current language states that churches and similar organizations "may not participate in, or intervene in (including the publishing or distributing of statements), any political campaign on behalf of (or in opposition to) any candidate for public office."[10] They must give impartial representation to all political entities in a given election or campaign.

Utilize Existing Church Documents

Many churches and denominations have existing statements on racial justice and racial reconciliation. Yet often these become zombie documents living somewhere on the web or in an office file cabinet. They may as well be dead documents when it comes to affecting change. Merely making the statement or a one-time act of putting words to the idea of racial justice is never enough. For these documents to have any power, they must reflect and inform the living narrative of a congregation or organization.

Churches can also do an entire preaching or teaching series based on denominational documents regarding race relations. They can take the Scripture passages cited in the documents and compose lessons about race relations based on those passages. Some church leaders may decide to host a special event around a particular document that can include a keynote address, panel discussion, or time for questions and answers.

One of the most significant ways a church can commit to racial justice is by taking an approved statement and forming a local congregational committee to determine how best to implement the ideas and recommendations contained in the document. Such an effort provides specificity to a universal document and involves the local congregation in the work of racial justice with the imprimatur of a larger ecclesiastical body.

Host a Freedom School

In 1964, the Council of Federated Organizations (COFO) coordinated the Mississippi Freedom Summer Project, otherwise known as Freedom Summer. This initiative brought hundreds of volunteers, many of them white college students from the North, to the state of Mississippi to help with voter registration. As part of the educational process, volunteers and local community activists hosted freedom schools.

Freedom schools taught academic skills and provided several tools necessary to pursue racial justice. These short-term schools were voluntary, and they took place in the summer when regular schools were not in session. They were staffed by volunteers who had been trained in a preapproved curriculum. Students ranged from elementary to high school, and many of the instructors were college students and young adults. The emphasis was on discussion rather than lecture and participation rather than passive consumption.[11]

Hosting a freedom school is still a great option for churches today, especially Black or other ethnic-specific churches that have already been engaged in the work for racial justice. Doing this well would, admittedly, be a significant undertaking involving the entire church or even multiple churches. Hosting a freedom school would involve creating curriculum, training instructors, and financial budgeting. But the effort would be similar to what many churches already do in hosting vacation Bible school or summer day camps, and the value it would bring to attendees would be immeasurable. In freedom schools, churches could educate young people about a biblical view of diversity, race, and ethnicity. They could explain the responsibility of Christians to love their neighbors in various ways, including working for equal rights for people of all races and ethnicities. Freedom schools should be attuned to the specific context of the local community. Upcoming elections, ballot measures, and issues of contention across racial lines should be explained and discussed. The goal of a school like this is not to inculcate students to support a particular candidate or party but to inform them about matters that affect their lives and instill from a young age a sense of collective responsibility for their community.

A freedom school could be structured similar to a summer day camp schedule, lasting about a week and serving the local population, especially students of color. To work best, the church should already have a presence in the community or be in a position to quickly build trust. One way to do this is by enlisting community members in the planning and preparation for the freedom school. You can canvas the neighborhood or approach civic organizations to share the idea, and then ask for volunteers from the community or for additional ideas from local residents. In poorer communities, matters such as food and transportation must also be addressed, and providing vans or buses as well as a meal or two will increase the likelihood that students will be able to participate. Bring in guest speakers such as the mayor, city council members, civil rights

activists, nonprofit leaders, and others to give short presentations and practical advice. Some full-time teachers may even
be willing to volunteer to help teach or form freedom school
curriculum over the summer. Instead of hosting a freedom
school, white churches should consider providing financial
resources and support personnel to Black churches and other
congregations led by people of color.

Start a Community Development Corporation

Churches cannot do everything necessary for justice to
flourish in a particular community. So much work needs to
be done that such endeavors could easily take up the majority
of church leaders' and members' time. Yet this is not a reason
to disengage from matters of racial justice in the community.
Many churches have started community development corporations (CDC) to foster justice in their neighborhoods and
cities. A community development corporation is a nonprofit
organization formed to meet the needs of the local community.
It typically has its own staff and recruits its own volunteers,
but many of the personnel, including board members, come
from the sponsoring church or churches. CDCs engage in a
wide spectrum of activities including educational enrichment,
sports, affordable housing, job training, physical and mental healthcare, and more. Whatever your community needs,
a CDC can be part of the solution.

In 1985, Pastor Tony Evans of Oak Cliff Bible Fellowship
in Dallas, Texas, established a CDC called the Turn Around
Agenda (then called Project Turnaround). Their mission is to
"rebuild communities from the inside out with comprehensive, faith-based programs and community partnerships that
transform the lives of urban youth and families."[12] Over the
years, its programs have grown to include a food pantry, K–12
public school outreach, a resale store, pregnancy services, and
training in computer and technology. Your church's CDC need
not be as comprehensive as the Turn Around Agenda; a small
start is sufficient to make a big impact. Begin by learning

from people who live in the neighborhood of the church. Go door-to-door and ask what people like about their community and what they want to change. Ask how a local church could be a positive presence for the people, businesses, and schools in the area. Never presume you know what residents of a community want or what assistance they may need. The best CDCs empower local residents to be part of the transformation in their own communities, and this begins by making their concerns your concerns.

Starting a CDC is a massive undertaking requiring legal expertise, establishing a board of directors, hiring an executive director, recruiting, training, and coordinating volunteers, and more. I advise churches to consider partnering with other churches or organizations to establish a CDC and share the workload. If starting your own CDC or working with other churches to begin one is not a viable option, then a church can also donate to existing community development projects and organizations. White churches can provide an especially valuable contribution by financially supporting a minority-led CDC initiative. Establish an annual line item in your budget to make supporting a community development corporation a regular part of the church's budget and vision.

Sponsor a School

As a former middle school teacher and principal, I know firsthand that public K–12 schools have immense needs, and churches can help. Many are underfunded, lack enough experienced teachers, and have a paucity of music and arts programs. They need all the support they can get! This need is even more acute when taking into account that the majority of Black students and other students of color attend public schools.

Churches can help by partnering with schools in a variety of ways. First, start by reaching out to school personnel, including the school board and local school principals. Ask what they perceive as the critical needs of the school or the local education system more broadly. Again, do not presume to know what people need without asking them. Yet as different as schools are from one another, there are some consistent patterns. Schools can almost always benefit from mentors and volunteers. Students at any grade level need people who will give them attention, care, and affirmation. Mentoring programs allow adults to provide tutoring, enrichment experiences such as field trips and other excursions, as well as the personal presence everyone needs in order to feel loved. A church can also organize a book drive for local schools. Congregations can agree to solicit donations from congregation and community members and then give those books to the local school or to individual students. Churches can help provide enrichment activities and programs that schools may not be able to provide because of a lack of funding. Depending on the skills and personnel in your congregation, you can start or coach a sports team, offer lessons in musical instruments, start a drama club and produce a play, sponsor a hobby-focused club such as chess or gaming, or teach a second language.

The adults involved in public education also need care and support. Teachers and administrators work hours that extend beyond the normal school day. They make crafts and design activities. They use their own money to provide classroom supplies. They use their "vacation" time to lesson plan, grade, and check in on students. Churches can support the adults involved in education in a variety of ways. Give gift certificates for massages, pay for mental health care or other self-care activities, order food for lunch or after work. Even something as simple as getting a group of church members together to support and boost the audience of a school event demonstrates commitment and gratitude for educators and all they do for their students. Also, don't forget the staff and administrators. Classroom teachers tend to be the focus of service activities, but there is an entire infrastructure of personnel beyond the classroom who need care too.

The opportunities for getting involved in local public schools run long, and the need is urgent. The primary concern in doing this should be to serve the school and the students, but there is also great value for the church as well. Few institutions are rooted in the community as deeply as public schools. If you want to better know your neighborhood, your city, and the people in it, getting involved in schools is one of the best ways to do it. Spending an hour with a student during tutoring or taking time to listen to teachers and principals can provide more helpful information than any book or article. Developing meaningful personal relationships with local educators and students can open you up to more cross-cultural interaction than any one-time presentation or discussion. Any church dedicated to racial justice must consider how they can support and invest in their local public schools.

Every church has the opportunity to pursue racial justice in its local context. How has God uniquely positioned your group to participate in the positive transformation of your community? In what ways can your congregation exercise spiritual imagination to break down the walls of bigotry and build bridges of equity? The entire Bible and the life of Jesus Christ testify that the witness of the Christian life is one of both word and deed. This witness is the proclamation that God offers salvation to all who repent and believe and that this good news extends not just to our spiritual state but to our material condition as well. The question is not *if* churches should work for racial justice but *how* they should do so.

Chapter 9

HOW TO FIGHT SYSTEMIC RACISM

For many young Black people, the killing of eighteen-year old Black teenager Mike Brown by a white police officer in Ferguson, Missouri, catalyzed their convictions to commit to antiracist actions. I am one of those people. My resolve to fight for racial justice increased in the months following the killing. Although I had already been involved in racial reconciliation efforts in my church and through my writing, my attention shifted from increasing interracial understanding through relationships to working for systemic and institutional change.

As protests mounted around the country, like many others I tried to make sense of the situation. Drawing heavily on the work of historians, I realized that fighting racism necessitates working for change beyond an interpersonal level; substantive change requires shifts at the institutional and policy level too.

Black people comprise 70 percent of Ferguson's population. That large number is not by coincidence.[1] Residential segregation had been a practice in the St. Louis–area as early as 1916. Harland Bartholomew, a city planning engineer at the time said one goal of these zoning practices was "to prevent movement into 'finer residential districts . . . by people of color.'"[2] This was reinforced by federal commissions and the National Association of Real Estate Boards, and residential segregation persisted into the late twentieth century. The flight of white people from racially transitioning neighborhoods, the gentrification of urban areas, and highway reroutings forced the city's Black residents to relocate to different areas of the city. The famous Gateway Arch landmark in St. Louis was constructed by demolishing existing neighborhoods, many of which were predominantly Black, and this displaced those residents to inner-ring suburbs like Ferguson.[3]

In addition to the concentration of low-income Black people in communities such as Ferguson, the police force subjected residents to harsh patrolling and penalties. In the aftermath of Mike Brown's death, the Department of Justice scrutinized the Ferguson Police Department and found a pattern of anti-Black discrimination. "Data collected by the Ferguson Police Department from 2012 to 2014 shows that African Americans account for 85% of vehicle stops, 90% of citations, and 93% of arrests made by FPD officers, despite comprising only 67% of Ferguson's population."[4] Ferguson's municipal leaders saw the fines and fees issued by police officers as a source of revenue and directed law enforcement to impose stricter policing as a way to balance the budget. As a result, "Partly as a consequence of City and FPD priorities, many officers appear to see some residents, especially those who live in Ferguson's predominantly African American neighborhoods, less as constituents to be protected than as potential offenders and sources of revenue."[5]

Researching the historical context of Ferguson helped me better understand why the fatal encounter between Mike Brown and a white police officer was not a question of "if" but "when." It also helped me to understand why the claim that racial discrimination in policing was the result of the individual prejudice of specific officers—the "one bad apple" defense—does not adequately explain decades of police brutality and numerous killings of unarmed Black people. As far back as the 1968 Kerner Commission report on urban unrest, analysts concluded, "To some Negroes police have come to symbolize white power, white racism, and white repression. And the fact is that many police do reflect and express these white attitudes."[6] Residential segregation, abusive policing practices, and generational poverty—these inequalities cannot be attributed to the actions of a few individuals or supposed pathologies of people of color. The reason we face widespread racial inequality today is due to systems—political, educational, cultural, economic—that have been set up to support it.

Philosopher and theologian Cornel West has said, "Justice is what love looks like in public."[7] The logical extension of the Christian ethic of love is advocacy for the public good, and this is accomplished not just through our individual actions but through collective efforts at systemic change. The ARC of Racial Justice reminds us that just as individuals can act in racist ways, institutions can develop policies and practices that are racially discriminatory. When racist policies of different institutions intersect and interact, they create systemic racism. This chapter outlines several ways to fight this systemic racism, and it often involves large-scale changes in the way we structure elements of society.

Essential Understandings

It Is Not Just about Individual Behavior

Acknowledging the reality of systemic racism means that we also acknowledge that a person's hardships are not *merely* due to their actions. Some believe that people are poor because they are lazy or unmotivated. A poll conducted by the *Washington Post* and the Kaiser Family Foundation revealed that 53 percent of white evangelical Protestants blamed poverty on a lack of effort. Compare this to 64 percent of Black Christians who attribute poverty more to circumstances. This divide over the cause of poverty is politically partisan as well. "Among Democrats, 26 percent blamed a lack of effort and 72 percent blamed circumstances. Among Republicans, 63 percent blamed lack of effort and 32 percent blamed circumstances."[8] These data show that many groups still think of society-wide issues such as poverty in individualist terms, as a matter that depends more on personal behaviors than policies and systems. William Darity Jr. and A. Kirsten Mullen, in their book on reparations, *From Here to Equality*, explain that "positive effort, strong motivation, and high academic achievement never have been sufficient to eliminate disparities in racial economic well-being, security, and opportunity."[9] What is needed in the fight against racism is a focus that takes into account the individual's circumstances while also taking action to combat the underlying systemic injustice.

One way to do this is to think about the effect of policies. In the book *How to Be an Antiracist*, Ibram X. Kendi explains that a racist policy is "any measure that produces or sustains racial inequality between racial groups," and he defines a policy to include "written and unwritten laws, rules, procedures, processes, regulations, and guidelines that govern people."[10] There is no such thing as a race-neutral policy. Every policy is "producing or sustaining either racial inequity or equity between racial groups."[11] For example, consider that under the 1986 Anti-Drug Abuse Act, which was finally revised in 2010, federal policy required a five-year mandatory minimum sentence for defendants found with just five grams of crack cocaine. But that five-year penalty was only triggered at 500 grams for powder cocaine. Same drug, different forms, yet a 100:1 sentencing disparity. On its face, this law has nothing to do with race. But there was racial bias embedded in the law. "Because of its relative low cost, crack cocaine is more accessible for poor Americans, many of whom are African Americans. Conversely, powdered cocaine is much more expensive and tends to be used by more affluent white Americans."[12] Fighting racism means looking at the operating system of our society and evaluating which protocols are creating or perpetuating racial injustice.

It Is about Impact, Not Intent

In most legal proceedings, the plaintiff has to prove that racial discrimination was the motivating factor behind the creation and implementation of a certain policy. This is a high, often impossible standard because it requires verifiable evidence of a person or a group's intent to discriminate based on race, something like a recorded phone call, an email, a memo, or eyewitness testimony where the perpetrators demonstrated racist motivations. The problem is that even overt racists know enough to conceal their beliefs, and even if such evidence is found, one can easily claim, "I didn't mean to be racist!" In many professional organizations and in politics, the difficulty of proving racist intent means that almost nothing is ever deemed racist.

Instead of focusing on intent, more attention should be paid to the impact or outcome of an action. If the result of a particular policy is to generate or sustain racial inequality, then such a policy might be racist. Racial justice advocates must recognize that, while intent matters, impact is what is critical in evaluating the fairness of a rule or practice. We must look at outcomes to evaluate whether a policy moves us further toward racial justice or further from it.

What Is Worth Conserving?

This chapter may be difficult for those who consider themselves politically conservative. But just as we should not pursue certain solutions simply because they are new, we should not preserve patterns simply because they are familiar. When it comes to political policies as they relate to race, we should ask the question: What is worth conserving?

From the earliest days of the United States, racism and white supremacy have been codified in official laws and policies. Article I, Section II, of the US Constitution originally declared that enslaved Black people would count only as three-fifths of a (white) person in the formula to determine state population for taxation and representation purposes. The Dred Scott decision of 1857 declared that Black people were "an inferior order, and altogether unfit to associate with the white race" and that Black people "had no rights which the white man was bound to respect."[13] Until recently, states such as Florida had a lifetime ban on voting for convicted felons even after they had served their sentence.[14] Because of racial bias in policing and arrests, laws curtailing the vote had the most harmful ramifications on racial and ethnic minorities.

When racial inequality gets inscribed into policy those policies must change. Racial progress in the political realm necessarily implies "progressive" policies. Even though "progressive" has taken on a political and cultural significance all its own, in this context it simply means progressing beyond the harmful rules and practices that create and maintain racial inequality. Wherever you fall on the political spectrum from conservative to progressive, we should be able to agree that doing the same things that got us here will not move us further down the path of racial justice.

Racial Justice Practices

Advocate for Voting Rights

In 2018, Stacey Abrams became the first Black female to run as the gubernatorial candidate of one of the two major parties. A Yale-trained lawyer and a Democrat, Abrams had served in the Georgia House of Representatives from 2007 to 2017 and was the minority leader for most of that time. Many speculate that Abrams might have become the first Black woman in US history to serve as a governor had it not been for the suppression of voting rights.

Abrams' opponent, Brian Kemp, was also the Secretary of State for Georgia during the campaign. His office had the responsibility of administering and monitoring the elections. In a clear conflict of interest, Kemp had the power to influence the election in a way that favored his chances of winning—a bit like serving as both the referee and a player in a tennis match. From 2012 to 2018, Kemp's office cancelled more than 1.4 million voter registrations, and nearly half of those cancellations occurred in 2017, in what he called "voter roll maintenance." Then, in the months immediately preceding the November 2018 gubernatorial election, the Secretary of State office held up 53,000 pending voter registration applications. Kemp implemented an "exact match" policy where a registration could be put on hold if a name on an application did not exactly match state records. So, for example, someone's application could be put on hold for a missing hyphen or for a typo. Most of the applications on the list of holds consisted of Black voters who tend to vote for Democrats. While 32 percent of Georgia's population is Black, the list of registrations on hold was nearly 70 percent Black.[15] These factors, combined with closing or relocating local precincts, ostensibly as cost-saving measures, more than doubled the average distance a Georgian had to travel to vote between 2012 and 2018, and Black people were 20 percent less likely to vote because of these distances.[16] Georgia is just one example of a broader trend. Even with automatic voter registration and mail-in voting options, exercising the right to vote has become increasingly difficult, especially for racial and ethnic minorities. Despite our long history of civil-rights activism, the democratic principle of "one person, one vote" remains in peril today.

Yet voting is a civically sacred right and duty. The sad reality is that Native Americans, Black people, and women have all been subject to disfranchisement at some point in our history. As far back as the nineteenth century and immediately following the Civil War, states attempted to disfranchise certain voters. Congress ratified the Fifteenth Amendment in 1870 to ensure that no one could be denied the right to vote based on "race, color or previous condition of servitude." Yet state legislators, especially in the South, had other plans. They passed laws that instituted poll taxes, understanding clauses, and literacy tests such as the one Fannie Lou Hamer endured in order to exclude Black people from voting. These forms of voter repression made ensuring the voting rights of all people a key demand of the Civil Rights movement of the 1950s and 1960s.

Even today some legislators and courts continue to roll back voter protections. In 2013, the Supreme Court passed down the *Shelby County v. Holder* decision which struck down a key provision of the Voting Rights Act. In 1965 when the Voting Rights Act passed, section 5 mandated "preclearance" for any changes in voting rules in areas that had a record of racially discriminatory voting policies. These areas had to get permission to change their voting laws to ensure that they would not continue their record of voter disfranchisement. In 2013, the Supreme Court determined that section 4(b), which contained the formula for determining which regions had to obtain preclearance, was invalid and unconstitutional. Writing the majority opinion, Chief Justice John Roberts stated, "The formula captures States by reference to literacy tests and low voter registration and turnout in the 1960s and early 1970s. But such tests have been banned for over 40 years."[17] Essentially, the argument was that the preclearance provision had worked so well that it was no longer needed. But in striking down the rule, justices effectively removed a key tool that ensured states would not resurrect voter suppression practices in the future. Writing the dissent, Justice Ruth Bader Ginsburg stated, "Throwing out preclearance when it has worked and is continuing to work to stop discriminatory changes is like throwing away your umbrella in a rainstorm because you are not getting wet."[18]

Since the Supreme Court issued their ruling in *Shelby v. Holder*, nearly 1,000 polling places have been closed, many of them in the majority Black counties of southern states.[19] Within months after the ruling, lawmakers in North Carolina initiated a new raft of voting restrictions that would eventually be passed into law. The new rules mandated strict voter ID laws, restricted early voting, did away with same-day registration, and included other provisions that made it more difficult to register.[20] Each of these measures disproportionately and negatively impact racial and ethnic minorities and the poor. In 2016, the Fourth Circuit Court of Appeals struck down North Carolina's new restrictions on voting for several reasons. While the new laws were ostensibly passed to prevent voter fraud, numerous studies have shown the incidence of fraud in elections is exceedingly rare. One study found only 31 cases of voter impersonation out of 1 billion votes.[21] The court also discovered that, in preparation to write the bill, the legislature requested data about the use of various voting practices *according to race.* They used this racial data to enact voting laws targeting the voting methods Black voters were most likely to employ. In the court's decision, Justice Diana Gribbon Motz wrote, "The new provisions target African Americans with almost surgical precision."[22]

In the twenty-first century, the long struggle to secure and protect the voting rights of Black people and other people of color continues. Legislators across the nation have devised savvy and subtle ways to get their preferred candidates elected, even if this means preventing certain demographic groups from voting in large numbers. They close polling places in minority communities, move polling places to inconvenient locations, purge voter rolls based on specious criteria, and curtail registration and early voting provisions.

Fighting racism includes a commitment to protect the right of racial and ethnic minorities to vote. Look up the voting laws in your state. Pay special attention to any laws enacted after the 2013 *Shelby v. Holder* decision. You can advocate for the restoration of the preclearance provision of the Voting Rights Act. Additionally, since racial and ethnic minorities have a disproportionately large presence in the criminal justice system, racial justice advocates should promote laws to restore voting rights to the formerly incarcerated. In 2018, Floridians passed a ballot measure that restored voting rights to those convicted of a felony and who had completed all the terms of their sentence. This amendment restored the vote to over 1 million people.[23] Two states, Maine and Vermont, even permit incarcerated people to vote from prison.

During local, state, and national elections, you can become

an observer and report any measures that make it harder for people to vote. In addition, you can ensure that people who are eligible to vote are registered through voter registration rallies and drives. You can also help people on election days by providing transportation, information, and other support to ensure that voters get to the polls.

Voter turnout in the United States trails other democracies around the world. A survey by Pew Research found that turnout in the November 2016 presidential election in the United States was about 56 percent. Sweden, which has a compulsory voting law, has a turnout near 90 percent. Other countries without such laws, such as South Korea, have a turnout near 80 percent.[24] Fortunately, we already know which initiatives prove most helpful in untangling the sometimes labyrinthine process of voting. Policies that make it more convenient to vote include same-day registration and automatic registration when a person turns eighteen years old. Mail-in ballots took on heightened importance in the wake of the novel coronavirus pandemic of 2020 as the measure became a matter of health. Many nations hold elections on the weekend when more people are not working rather than on a weekday. Another popular suggestion is to make election day a federal holiday. For more information about voting and voting rights, you can visit your local Secretary of State's website or explore the voting guides produced by advocacy groups such as the NAACP. None of these initiatives will absolutely guarantee a higher voter turnout, but at a minimum they can make voting simpler and more accessible to more people.

Work for Immigration Reform

In April of 2018, the Trump Administration instituted a "zero tolerance" policy for all people who attempted to enter the United States unlawfully. This meant that legal entities in the United States would charge everyone who did not have the proper authorization with a crime. Previously prosecutors had some discretion about who to charge with a crime. The zero

tolerance policy meant that adults who had children with
them were separated, a practice commonly known as "family
separation."[25]

The policy sparked outrage as people worldwide saw pictures
of despondent children languishing without their parents in
sparse detention facilities. The deportation of undocumented
immigrants also aroused public debate and anger. President
Obama earned the nickname from some activists of "deporter
in chief" for the three million immigrants deported under his
administration.[26] In his second term Obama administration
officials made a point to prioritize the removal of immigrants
who had committed a crime.[27] Under the Trump administration, however, removals became indiscriminate.[28] While the
issue of harsh immigration practices is long-standing, and
both Democratic and Republican administrations have exac-
erbated the problem, the recent policy shifts have amplified a
contentious debate about immigration into the United States
and how to address the many people who do not have proper
documentation to be in the country while also treating them
and their families humanely.

To improve the situation for immigrants, our language
matters. Many activists and relief organizations strongly
advise against using the term *illegal immigrants.* "While a
person's mode of entry may be illegal, that does not define
their personhood, any more than someone who speeds on the
highway is 'an illegal.'" A more common and respectful term
is "undocumented."[29]

One major policy reform to consider is the protection of the
Deferred Action for Childhood Arrivals act (DACA). The policy
"grants undocumented immigrants brought to the United
States as children permission to live and work lawfully."[30]
Some legislators seek to strike down the DACA provisions,
which would put young people who have spent most or all
of their lives in the United States at risk of being sent to a
country that is unfamiliar to them. Even if their parents came
to the country unlawfully, young people who did not have a

choice in the matter should have a way to stay in the country without fear of deportation. Other immigration reforms include creating a pathway to citizenship that would allow current undocumented immigrants to engage in a process to become documented citizens. Some activists propose extending healthcare to undocumented immigrants, closing detention centers, and even abolishing the Immigration and Customs Enforcement (ICE) department.[31]

As with most policy changes, you can begin by making your opinions known to state and federal officials through phone calls, messages, and letters. In addition, immigration, especially processes such as seeking asylum and refugee status, can be nearly impossible to navigate without legal representation. Donating to organizations like the Immigrant Justice Corps can help.[32] Other organizations such as World Relief help raise awareness and provide direct assistance to immigrants.[33]

Pay Reparations to Black People

The devastating novel coronavirus pandemic in 2020 resulted in an action that many in the United States thought the federal government would never do: it wrote checks directly to citizens. While the initiative had widespread support from Democrats, many of whom wanted an even more robust package, even Senate majority leader Mitch McConnell said, "Senate Republicans want to put cash in the hands of the American people."[34] Congress passed a two trillion dollar economic stimulus bill in March 2020, the largest in US history, in order to provide relief to small businesses and individuals who could not work due to social distancing measures. Part of the package included direct payments to eligible people up to $1,200 per adult and $500 per child.[35] The exigencies of the coronavirus crisis highlighted the federal government's indispensable and irreplaceable role to work for the common good.

The 2020 stimulus bill, also known as the CARES Act, proves that it is possible for the United States to provide direct financial payments to individuals in cases of extreme economic hardship. Black Americans have faced extreme economic hardship in the United States since their ancestors were first brought over on slave ships. Slavery, at its most basic level, was an economically exploitative system that boosted the profits of plantation owners by depriving enslaved African laborers of wages. They spent countless hours laboring in sweltering heat only to retreat to sparse quarters at the end of the day and start all over again the next morning. This was the reality day-after-day and generation-after-generation. The economic exploitation of Black people did not end with emancipation however. How does one calculate the opportunities lost when families did not receive land of their own to begin building generational wealth? What about all the loans denied to Black people when they tried to purchase homes or get funding to start new businesses? What about the promotions white employers denied to Black people because they could not fathom a Black person being a white person's boss? Reparations are not simply about what happened during slavery; they are about the debt owed to Black people for the economic disadvantages created by white supremacy before, during, and since the practice of race-based chattel slavery.

At no time since the abolition of slavery has the nation ever made any widespread and sustained effort to financially compensate Black people for the theft of their labor. It did not happen in the years immediately following the Civil War when the formerly enslaved could be directly paid. And it has only gotten more complicated and less likely in the decades since. To this day, Black people still struggle to overcome the financial effects of the enslavement of their ancestors. A 2016 report by the Survey of Consumer Finances revealed that the median household wealth of Black families is just one-tenth the wealth of white households.[36] Another report found that the gap between white households and Black and Latino households is actually increasing and will get bigger if nothing is done. "If average Black family wealth continues to grow at the same pace it has over the past three decades, it would take Black families 228 years to amass the same amount of wealth White families [had in 2013]." To put that time frame in perspective, "That's just 17 years shorter than the 245-year span of slavery in this country," the report states. It would take Latinos 84 years to gain the same level of wealth that white families had in 2013.[37]

Any serious racial justice efforts must consider the financial effects of racism. Reparations, which simply means "repair," is one way to address the wealth gap due to racism. In the book *From Here to Equality: Reparations for Black Americans in the Twenty-First Century*, William "Sandy" Darity Jr. and A. Kirsten Mullen, two of the most prominent advocates of federal reparations, define reparations as "a program of acknowledgment, redress, and closure for a grievous injustice."[38] They further specify that in the case of African Americans reparations includes the economic costs associated with "slavery, legal segregation (Jim Crow), and ongoing discrimination and stigmatization."[39]

Economists and other experts have devised a variety of models to calculate the exact dollar amount of what would be owed to Black Americans in the present day. Darity and Mullen emphasize that any model for reparations must seek to close the racial wealth gap "because wealth (or net worth) is the most powerful indicator of the intergenerational effects of white supremacy on black economic well-being."[40] They base their model for calculating reparations on the value of the forty acres that freed Black people did not get after the Civil War:

Setting the size of the reparations fund can begin with a calculation of today's value of those long-ago promised 40 acres. The most conservative estimate of the total amount of land that should have been allocated to the 4 million freedmen is 40 million acres. The present value of an overall land grant of that size is approximately $1.5 to $2 trillion. If there are about 35 million black Americans who would be eligible for reparations, this minimum (or baseline) estimate would amount to $40,000 to $60,000 per person.[41]

Payments could be made in a lump sum or spread out over a period of years. In order to prove their ancestry and avoid people attempting to exploit the system for cash Darity and Mullen recommend two criteria. "First, U.S. citizens would need to establish that they had at least one ancestor who was enslaved in the United States after the formation of the republic."[42] The second factor is "they would have to prove that they self-identified as 'black,' 'Negro,' 'Afro-American,' or 'African American' *at least twelve years before* the enactment of the reparations program."[43]

While some may resist the idea of paying cash reparations, it should be noted that governments, including the United States, have done something similar in the past. Germany has paid about $50 billion to Holocaust survivors and their families. Japanese-Americans confined to internment camps during World War II received an apology from the government and $20,000 per victim.[44] No dollar amount can compensate for the discrimination and suffering Jewish people and Japanese Americans endured, but these historical examples serve as precedent for reparations to Black people.

No attempt to secure reparations for Black Americans can start without support from the public and Congress. As a start, advocates can support H.R. 40, the "Commission to Study and Develop Reparation Proposals for African-Americans Act," which is a bill to establish a federal study committee on reparations to African Americans. The commission will "examine (1) the role of federal and state governments in supporting the institution of slavery, (2) forms of discrimination in the public and private sectors against freed slaves and their descendants, and (3) lingering negative effects of slavery on living African-Americans and society."[45] John Conyers, of the US House of Representatives, first introduced the bill in 1989.

After thirty years of little traction for the bill, Congress finally held a hearing about reparations on Juneteenth of 2019.

Racial justice advocates can accelerate the process of paying reparations by bringing attention to the issue. Supporting the study committee is a first step. Calling and writing letters to Senators and Representatives in support of reparations is another. Voting for candidates who support reparations is a way to use your vote to close the racial wealth gap.

How Individuals and Organizations Can Pay Reparations

The fight for racial justice cannot wait for the federal government to act. Individuals and organizations can also take reparative steps on their own initiative. The elders and the congregation of Watermark Church in Tampa, Florida, have taken steps toward this, including hiring locally owned Black businesses for service contracts and for church events. When a local Black pastor who is friends with Watermark's senior pastor shared that their church was seven months and nearly $40,000 behind on rent, the leaders of Watermark Church voted to let them share Watermark's facilities at no cost. All of this is in addition to intentionally forming a racially and ethnically diverse leadership team and making racial justice a core characteristic of their church.[46]

Even though Historically Black Colleges and Universities (HBCUs) comprise just three percent of all colleges and universities, they produce 20 percent of all Black graduates. Twenty-five percent of all Black students with a degree in Science, Technology, Engineering, and Math (STEM) graduate from HBCUs. Yet many HBCUs face staffing and program cuts and even closure due to chronic underfunding.[47] Organizations and individuals can take up special collections or hold fundraisers to fund HBCUs or offer Black students scholarships and grants to attend HBCUs as an act of reparations.

When Radio Kingston put on the "Fall Fling" concert in Kingston, Jamaica, they and their partner organization, Rise Up, offered reparations pricing for tickets. While the event was free, the organizers invited white participants to voluntarily pay $10.79 (the radio station's call sign was 107.9) to cover the costs of their attendance and that of Black attendees.[48] Offering an optional reparations price for events and products helps Black-led organizations become more financially sustainable. At the very least, proposing such pricing will generate some lively discussion.

When I started The Witness, a Black Christian Collective, we had no money at all. To this day, most of our team are volunteers whose only compensation is the satisfaction of being part of an initiative that is meaningful to them. With more funding, we could not only pay our staff but also pay writers who contribute to our blog, buy equipment to improve our multimedia presence through podcasting and video production, finance staff retreats to create more content, and much more. After several years, when we finally began to engage in concerted fundraising efforts, we quickly discovered that we did not have the professional or social networks that many white evangelical institutions had to help them raise significant sums of money. Fundraising for a nonprofit is always difficult work, but when you are part of a historically marginalized group, it's even harder. Financially supporting Black-led organizations and ministries can help these groups continue to function and significantly improve the work they do.

While there is no substitute for financial contributions, one might also consider "in-kind" contributions that come in the form of service or expertise. As we attempted to secure official 501(c)3 nonprofit status at The Witness, white people volunteered their accounting and legal experience to help us get started. That saved us nearly $1,000. Other perennial needs for small, minority-led nonprofits include graphic design, grant writing, and fundraising. If you have specialized skills or training, offering pro bono services can be helpful to underfunded and minority-led organizations.

Reparations can take many forms, and people can sometimes surprise you with their financial generosity and creativity. After video emerged of the murder of Ahmaud Arbery, a Black man who had been pursued and killed by two white men while he was out for a jog, The Witness hosted a special conversation for our constituents online via Zoom.[49] We are blessed to have many white advocates who wanted to hear members of our team process this traumatic event. But oftentimes, these conversations can get overwhelmed by white people asking questions and offering comments. In the limited time we have, these remarks from white people take time and attention away from the Black people at such events.

At the beginning of the conversation, we gently invited white people to make space for the Black people who tuned in because we do not always have the opportunity to process tragedies in public without people from outside of our communities shifting the focus. After the event, one sensitive white person sent our organization $100 with a note that it was for reparations and thanking us for letting her enter into such a racially sensitive space. She was not apologizing for her presence; she was merely recognizing that as a white person her attendance can alter the social and cultural dynamics in ways that may not be helpful to racial and ethnic minorities. Acts of spontaneous generosity demonstrate an awareness of the need for reparations and spur creativity in ways to offer financial redress.

Reparations is a controversial topic for some people. It shouldn't be. Reparations simply means repair. White supremacy has decimated Black wealth and opportunity. No sufficient remedies have been applied. People too often mistake the dismantling of certain discriminatory practices for progress. It is good that laws have been passed to ban racial segregation, permit interracial marriage, and establish holidays commemorating Civil Rights leaders. But this is not reparations. As Malcolm X put it, "If you stick a knife in my back nine inches and pull it out six inches, there's no progress. If you pull it all the way out, that's not progress. Progress is healing the wound that the blow made."[50] The racial wealth gap is the bleeding wound of racism that will not heal apart from a comprehensive and substantive policy of financial reparations for Black people in America. Before asking about the complexity or popularity of reparations, first ask whether it is right. The past cannot be changed, but the future of wealth distribution is entirely up to us.

Criminal Justice Reform

In my third semester of graduate school, my department chairperson emailed me with a special opportunity. She asked if I was interested in being the teaching assistant for a class on African history. There was nothing too unusual about this request since I was required to assist in a class every semester. But what was different was that the class would take place in the Mississippi State Penitentiary, otherwise known as Parchman Farm, and the students would be incarcerated men. So for the next sixteen weeks I made the drive to Sunflower County in the heart of the Mississippi Delta. Parchman is the oldest prison in the state and it earned a notorious reputation for running as a plantation. White guards forced incarcerated Black men to clear the land and plant and harvest cotton. One historian of the prison wrote, "The convict's condition [following the Civil War] was much worse than slavery. The life of the slave was valuable to his master, but there was no financial loss . . . if a convict died."[51] Even though the prison has undergone many changes since its founding, it is still situated in the middle of sweltering fields that conjure up the days of slavery and sharecropping. Week after week, I got to know the men inside not as prisoners but as human beings with hopes, humor, intelligence, curiosity, and families. Many had broken the law and harmed others, but as lawyer and activist Bryan Stevenson often says, "Each of us is more than the worst thing we've ever done."[52]

Criminal justice reform is a pressing issue because of the stigma attached to incarceration. It is easy to assume that if people are guilty of a crime, then they deserve whatever punishments they receive behind bars. But it is important to remember that the process of ending up in prison is flawed and unfair at times. Extreme racial disparities exist that directly affect who gets put in prison. The Sentencing Project, a nonprofit group that works for a fair and effective criminal justice system finds that "African Americans are incarcerated in state prisons at a rate that is 5.1 times the imprisonment of whites."[53] Latinos are imprisoned at between 1.4 and 4.3 times the rate of white people depending on the state. Despite making up just 13 percent of the overall US population, Black people represent 38 percent of the incarcerated population.[54] In order to fight against racism on a systemic level, the criminal justice system must be overhauled. Activists propose an array of strategies for ensuring public safety and fair practices in the criminal justice system, but I want to highlight three.

First, we should abolish the death penalty. In 1944, fourteen-year-old George Stinney became the youngest person ever to have been executed in the United States. A newspaper article at the time described his last moments. "Guards had difficulty strapping the boy's slight form into place." Apparently, "he went calmly to the electric chair . . . with a Bible under his arm."[55] After a trial that lasted a single day, an all-white male jury deliberated for just ten minutes before deciding to convict young Stinney for allegedly murdering two white girls aged seven and eleven years old. Seventy years later, in 2014 a South Carolina judge vacated the decision, saying that Stinney had been denied his constitutional rights. His surviving siblings, who advocated the judicial reexamination, insisted their brother had been in the house during the murders and was innocent of all charges.[56]

Since 1973, more than 165 people sentenced to death row have been found innocent,[57] and from a racial standpoint, 42 percent of people on death row are Black.[58] The death penalty does not work as a deterrent to crime, and one in nine people on death row have been exonerated.[59] Executions cannot be undone. The victims of the death penalty are disproportionately Black, and some argue it is a cruel and unusual form of punishment.[60]

The United States remains part of a small number of nations worldwide that permit the death penalty. The tide, however, is changing. So far twenty-two states have abolished the death penalty, and more are considering it. Donate to organizations committed to abolishing the death penalty and call or write to your state and national representatives to let them know your opposition to the practice. To fight racism, we must join efforts to eliminate the death penalty and intervene in specific cases when individuals face imminent death by the state.

Second, eliminate cash bail and reform or eliminate solitary confinement. Kalief Browder was sixteen years old when a fellow New Yorker accused him of stealing a backpack with personal electronics and $700 cash in it. Journalist Jennifer Gonnerman wrote an extended article in the *New Yorker* in 2014 about Browder's ordeal.[61] In it she explains how Browder insisted he had not stolen the bag, and police searched him but did not find anything. They arrested him anyway on the assurance that he would likely be held just a few hours and then be released. Instead Browder, who was on probation for a previous and unrelated issue, was sent to jail on Rikers Island. A judge had set bail at $3,000, a sum his family couldn't afford.

Browder ended up spending over 1,000 days in jail awaiting trial. Nearly two years of that time was spent in solitary confinement where the young man attempted suicide several times. Lawyers and judges kept delaying his case until finally, the prosecutors dropped it altogether. But after his release Browder struggled with mental illness, and on June 6, 2015, he killed himself at his home.[62] In 2017, rapper Jay-Z helped produce a documentary called *Time: The Kalief Browder Story* about the young man's tragic experiences in the justice system.

Kalief Browder might still be alive today if we had eliminated cash bail from the criminal justice system. His case also brings up critical questions about the use of solitary confinement, especially for juveniles. While many states have passed reforms in the years since Browder's incarceration, you should check your state's department of corrections to find out about cash bail and solitary confinement. Bryan Stevenson has said, "We have a system of criminal justice that treats you better if you're rich and guilty than if you are poor and innocent."[63] This is true, but we can fight such injustices. Call your state representatives and senators to let them know you oppose the cash bail system and want to see measures that keep people out of jail during the pretrial phase as much as possible. While laws may take years to change, you can still help right now. Several charities dedicated to paying bail for accused people exist. You can donate to organizations such as the National Bail Fund Network and the Bail Project to help people get out of jail immediately and avoid the traumas and abuses of incarceration.

Third, we need to overhaul police practices. It may be difficult for white people to understand that to many Black people, the police are not a welcome presence. In the 1960s, activists in Oakland formed the Black Panther Party. But most people are likely not aware of their full name at the time they were founded: the Black Panther Party for Self-Defense. Members formed police patrols to monitor how police conducted themselves during encounters with local Black community members, and included in their "10-Point Platform" was the demand to reduce police brutality: "We want an immediate end to POLICE BRUTALITY and MURDER of black people."[64]

The murder of George Floyd in May 2020 brought the issue of anti-Black police brutality crashing into the broader national consciousness yet again. In the wake of the murder, activists called for much more sweeping changes in policing. Hashtags such as #AbolishthePolice and #DefundthePolice began trending on social media. Mariame Kaba, a leading voice in the police abolition movement, argues that reforms such as implicit bias training and tighter use-of-force policies do not effectively reduce the violence enacted by US-style policing. "Enough. We can't reform the police. The only way to diminish police violence is to reduce contact between the public and the police," wrote Kaba.[65]

A key element of abolishing the police is defunding the police. Angela Davis, an academic and an activist who has been involved in Black freedom struggles since the 1960s, explains that defunding the police is not just about taking funds away but redirecting them toward more effective measures that prevent the need for police in the first place. "It's about shifting public funds to new services and new institutions—mental health counselors, who can respond to people who are in crisis without arms. It's about shifting funding to education, to housing, to recreation. All of these things help to create security and safety."[66]

The police-related killings of unarmed Black people cry out for changes in the way law enforcement is conducted in this country. While we may differ on strategies, those strategies should be evaluated and debated and the most oppressed people should be at the heart of the conversation.[67] The most effective changes in the criminal justice system will reduce harm and increase the ability of communities to access the resources that prevent crime in the first place.

Promote Equitable Funding for Public Schools

In numerous ways, people with resources and racial privilege have sought to keep their schools separate from "those kids," which often refers to poor and working-class students and families of color. This has resulted in vastly unequal funding and educational outcomes between white students and students of color. This disparity is often referred to as the "achievement gap," but some have contended that it is more appropriately termed the "opportunity gap" since students of color have not been afforded the same opportunities as their white counterparts. People committed to racial justice must take the opportunity gap in public education as a central concern. Today over half of public education students attend racially segregated schools, defined as schools with 75 percent or more of students who are either white or nonwhite.[68] It cannot be acceptable in the twenty-first century that schools in many places are as segregated—or even more so—than they were in the 1950s and 1960s.

Racially segregated schools get vastly different funding. Public schools get their money through a combination of federal, state, and local sources with the majority of funds coming from the latter two. At the local level, property taxes determine the level of funding for particular schools. Boundaries for school districts are often drawn in such a way that more affluent districts are separated from poorer districts in both rural and urban areas. Thus one school district may receive more funds because they have more money from property taxes, while a district a short distance away may receive much less funding because the tax base is smaller.

Some school districts have achieved greater levels of racial integration by organizing schools according to grade level rather than geographic zones. Nearly half a century ago in the town of Clinton, Mississippi—immediately west of Jackson—officials made the decision to structure schools in their district in this way. Elementary-age students would go to one school, junior high students to another, and high schoolers to another school regardless of the location of their homes in the city.

Today Clinton Public Schools defy the trend of segregation. Of the over 5,000 students in the district, 54 percent are Black, 36 percent are white, six percent are Asian, two percent are Hispanic, and 2 percent are comprised of other racial and ethnic groups. Half the students are considered low-income. What's more, the school district consistently achieves an 'A' rating in the state's evaluation system and ranks as one of the top districts in a state notorious for its racial segregation and racism. It is not as if schools with a higher level of racial diversity have eliminated racism in their ranks—they still have plenty of problems. But such schools offer alternatives to the hypersegregation that characterize many places of learning.[69]

Equity in public education is the goal. Black people and

other people of color are not clamoring simply to sit next to white people. In fact, there are risks of changing the community dynamics of a majority-minority school with the introduction of white students and parents. Those places may become more fraught with racial tension or dilute their messages of uplift in an effort to avoid conflict. But there are benefits to racial integration. According to economist Philip Rucker, racial integration leads to higher income and more years of education for students of color. It also reduces racial prejudice among white students.[70] Fighting racism in public education requires racial justice advocates to push districts to redraw their boundaries to include poorer neighborhoods and ones with more students of color. Lawmakers must change policies that keep neighborhoods racially and economically segregated and thus result in segregated schools.

Much more could be mentioned—racial disparities in healthcare, the disproportionate effects of environmental degradation on communities of color, and continued discrimination in housing and real estate to name a few. There is no shortage of causes you can get involved in once you realize the systemic and institutional nature of racism. The "commitment" portion of the ARC of Racial Justice requires acknowledging that policies, not just the personal attitudes of individuals, perpetuate racism too. Those policies must be changed in order to promote racial justice. For too long the discussion about race has focused on the intentions and feelings of individuals, and this has allowed people to sidestep the necessity of addressing systemic racism. But confronting the interlocking pattern of practices and policies that create and maintain racial inequality is what love looks like in public.

Chapter 10

HOW TO ORIENT YOUR LIFE TO RACIAL JUSTICE

Although I grew up in the Midwest, I've spent my entire adult life in the Deep South, mainly in the Mississippi River Delta. I try not to draw stark lines between the South and other parts of the country because racism transcends regions, but the racial geography of the South does stand out. Many of the battles of the Civil War were fought there. The South was the main theater in which the Civil Rights movement was waged. As such, these lands carry within them the voices of the ancestors.

In Mississippi alone I have encountered the legacies of Fannie Lou Hamer, Medgar Evers, James Meredith, and Ida B. Wells, just to name a few. Living alongside the cotton fields where my forebears sharecropped or were enslaved, personally meeting civil rights leaders or those who knew them, and learning about the long history of fighting against racism instill in me a sense of deep resolve to continue in the tradition of racial justice activism. As I look to my ancestors, whose opportunities were far more limited than mine but who fought and persevered nonetheless, I cannot help but commit my very life to continuing their struggle.

Fighting racism does not consist of a set of isolated actions that you take; rather these actions must flow from an entire disposition that is oriented toward racial justice. We have to reposition ourselves spiritually, emotionally, culturally, intellectually, and politically to address the myriad ways that racism manifests in the present day. Racial justice is a life-style not an agenda item.

This chapter details the personal dimension of the Commitment portion of the ARC of Racial justice. It outlines the ways an individual can orient her or his life toward racial justice. Fighting for racial justice entails a daily compact with yourself and others who do this work never to quit when it gets hard or inconvenient. It is a commitment to living in such a way that your entire life is a witness for racial justice. It is difficult to live righteously when it comes to race, but in doing so you are creating a legacy. Orienting your life in this way is about helping to shape your society into one that might be more equitable and just today as well as for the generations that follow. It is about being a good ancestor.

Essential Understandings

Cancel Contempt

Contempt is the poison pill of racial justice. A distorted understanding of personhood leads to feelings of superiority or inferiority. People who act in racist ways can treat people of color with contempt, believing others are somehow less capable and more prone to error than they are. On the other side, racial justice advocates can quickly become contemptuous of those they view as racists and view themselves as superior because of their enlightenment or "wokeness." While one side has healthier beliefs about race than the other, contempt is never the answer.

Dr. John Gottman, one of the foremost experts on marriage and relationships, contends that contempt "arises from a sense of superiority over one's partner. It is a form of disrespect."[1] Forms of contempt include sarcasm, cynicism, name-calling, eye-rolling, mockery, and belligerence.[2] In a marriage, Gottman's research has found, contempt is the number one predictor of divorce.[3] The damaging effects of contempt apply not only to marriage but to racial justice as well. We must constantly check our hearts to ensure that we are not demonstrating contempt for others. The temptation to look down on others because of their backward views on race and diversity easily descends into disdain and haughtiness. Feelings of contempt dehumanize other people and cause us to replicate the hate we wish to eradicate. So to make racial justice a lifelong pursuit, we must constantly battle against any feelings of contempt we have toward other people.

Have This Mind Among Yourselves

According to a popular tale, *The Times* newspaper in London asked authors, "What's wrong with the world?" Famous author G. K. Chesterton responded, "Dear Sirs, I am."[4] Chesterton's succinct but pithy answer stays in circulation today because it articulates a profound truth: We are all part of the problem.

Philippians 2:3–4 says, "Do nothing out of selfish ambition or vain conceit. Rather, in humility value others above yourselves, not looking to your own interests but each of you to the interests of the others." This is the mindset we must have as we pursue racial justice as a way of life and not simply a pastiche of isolated actions. Fighting racism is ultimately about serving other people from a wellspring of love. A spirit of loving service has to be infused with a spirit of humility that puts the interests of others before our own.

To pursue racial justice, the critical attitude we must cultivate is humility—to listen and learn, yes, but also to admit that we, too, can act in racist ways. We must have the humility to realize that, in some cases, we have benefited from the racial status quo. White people must recognize with humility that, although life can be difficult for anyone, their skin color has not added to their hardships. People of color must recognize that, despite their life experiences, they can sometimes get it wrong when it comes to race.

When I served as the principal of a middle school, one of

my main jobs was ensuring the safety and learning of our students through effective classroom management. We had several first-year teachers, and almost no one is good at classroom management in their first year. One teacher who reported to me never looked at me when I gave her feedback. I thought this was curious, but I never mentioned it until one day when her behavior irked me. I was offering her some input on how to improve her teaching, and midway through my little speech I stopped and asked, "Could you at least look at me when I'm talking?" She did not say anything in the moment but went back to her class and did the best she could.

Later that day the teacher asked to see me in my office. She explained to me that as a person of Asian descent in her culture it was considered rude and disrespectful to look at an elder or a boss directly in the eyes. She was not trying to offend me. She was actually showing me respect. In response, I had shown ignorance and rudeness. I immediately apologized and thanked her for her courage and initiative to enlighten me. Anyone can get it wrong. And that's especially true when it comes to racial justice. The key is owning your mistakes, learning from them, and staying on the journey.

In Matthew 7, Jesus confronts those who would self-righteously judge the shortcomings of others while ignoring their own flaws. "Why do you look at the speck of sawdust in your brother's eye and pay no attention to the plank in your own eye?" (Matt. 7:3). In our journey toward racial justice, we must always self-monitor for the ways we are reenacting racism, even if unintentionally, and seek to correct our attitudes and behaviors. This must be done even as we observe the world around us and attempt to correct the injustices for which others are responsible. As Jesus put it, "You hypocrite, first take the plank out of your own eye, and then you will see clearly to remove the speck from your brother's eye" (Matt. 7:5).

White people must constantly cultivate humility in order to acknowledge their complicity in racism and engage in the process of repentance and repair. Racism is designed to be invisible to white people—this is just the way things are, or this is the "right" way to do things—so when they are confronted by the reality of racism, it can offend their sense of personal innocence. There is no way around this feeling. You have to go through a process of deconstructing the ways white supremacy has skewed your perception in order to see the reality of race more clearly.

For people of any race or ethnicity, humility is a key attitude in the work of racial justice. It takes humble honesty to consider one's shortcomings and still pursue the work of fighting racism. Humility allows new information to correct old ideas and leads us into better ways of loving one another. Humility forces us to descend from our lofty perches of self-justification to consider how our action or inaction can contribute to racism. Humility undergirds all the actions that orient one's life toward racial justice.

Keep the Light Switch On

There's a big difference between a light switch and a smoke alarm. A light switch can be turned on and off. A smoke alarm is always on. Racial justice for white people is often like a light switch. You can turn it on or off whenever you feel like it. But for people of color, racial justice is more like a smoke alarm. It always has to be on just to keep safe and avoid danger.

Every day, people of color in the United States are reminded that they are different or "other." They are reminded of their marginalized status when they try to hail a cab or use a ride share service, when someone tries to pronounce their name, when they are zoned for a particular school, when they receive a paycheck with a lower amount than their white peer, when they see another instance of police brutality enacted against someone who looks like them. By contrast, white people may never think about themselves or their neighbors in racial terms. What happens or does not happen to them seems to be entirely a consequence of chance and personal decisions. Race may hardly seem like a factor at all.

Since race affects white people and people of color so differently, one of the most important racial justice practices is to remain conscious of race even when you have the option of not doing so. For white people, this demonstrates genuine solidarity with people of color. The height of "faux alliance" is attuning to racial issues for a season or a moment and then going back to business as usual whenever conditions become inconvenient or uncomfortable. Racial justice is demonstrated not in the times when everyone is talking about race but in those times when it would be easy or expected to overlook race.

The only way to keep the racial justice light switch on is to set up structures and routines that make this possible. Do not rely on willpower alone. You can keep racial justice at the forefront by participating in groups—whether book studies, activist organizations, nonprofits, or otherwise—that make it a constant topic. Attending a church that makes racial justice a core commitment will keep the issue up front. Meaningful friendships and professional relationships with people of color will also make their concerns more salient to you on a day-to-day basis.

In the pages that follow, you will find racial justice practices that will help you orient your entire life around racial justice. In time, these practices will hone your racial reflexes so you can respond nimbly and adeptly to the various ways you will continue to encounter injustice.

Racial Justice Practices

Budget Your Time toward Racial Justice

The reasons more people do not actively purse racial justice can be deep and complex, but sometimes they are fairly simple. To practice racial justice, you must make time for it. It takes time to attend meetings, print fliers, make phone calls, participate in a march, read books, and do all the tasks necessary for a life of racial justice activism. Most of us have too much to do and too little time. The idea of allocating time for racial justice is not only impractical—it is overwhelming. Yet that is precisely what must be done.

Getting serious about fighting racism entails auditing how you spend your time and making room for justice concerns. Just as you have to revise your financial budget so you can make an important investment, you may have to shuffle your time and priorities to make investments in racial justice. You can start by looking at activities or organizations you want to engage with and estimating how much time you will need. Then look at your schedule to see how to make time for it. Between the hours many of us spend on social media or engaging in tasks that we should really delegate or say no to, we can find more time for racial justice if we are intentional. Also remember that racial justice consists not simply in external action but internal reflection as well. The time you spend thinking, praying, and processing is time that counts toward fighting racism too.

Give Sacrificially

The word *tithe* derives from a word meaning "a tenth." In the Bible, tithing means giving a portion of one's income or wealth to the work of God's kingdom. As far back as Genesis, Moses gave Melchizedek, the king of Salem, a tenth of everything he owned (Gen. 14:20). The Israelites were instructed to give a tenth of their resources to the maintenance of the temple and to support the Levites who tended the temple. The money was also to be used specifically to help the marginalized and oppressed. "When you have finished setting aside a tenth of all your produce in the third year, the year of the tithe, you shall give it to the Levite, the foreigner, the fatherless and the widow, so that they may eat in your towns and be satisfied," (Deut. 26:12). The people of God have a mandate to give a portion of their wealth to the work of justice.

But 10 percent serves as a minimum, not a maximum, for giving. What if you practiced "reverse tithing"—giving away 90 percent and keeping 10 percent to live on? After he graduated from college, Graham Smith secured a lucrative job as an investment banker on Wall Street. People in this profession can easily make a six-figure salary even in their first year. With performance and seniority, their salary increases, as do their bonuses.[5] But Smith remembered a warning from one of his professors about "Golden Handcuffs," the idea that one can be so tied to making money and living a materially comfortable life that it becomes a prison preventing you from doing what may be less lucrative but more beneficial to yourself and others.

Smith took this warning seriously, and instead of living luxuriously like many of his peers, he cultivated a simple lifestyle that enabled him to live off 10 percent of his income. He gave away the other 90 percent, in effect, reversing the typical tithing numbers. In 2017, Smith and his wife opened P. S. Kitchen—a vegan restaurant that employs the formerly incarcerated and homeless—and they donate 100 percent of the profit to charitable work.[6]

Not everyone has the luxury of a salary large enough to give away most of their income and still support themselves, but the principle of generous, sacrificial giving is universal. Instead of donating the barest amount possible, what are ways you or your organization can give radically and sacrificially? In the previous chapter we discussed reparations and what it might look like to support racial and ethnic minorities with your finances. Those efforts focused on what the federal government and other organizations could do to help close the racial wealth gap and address the hardships it produces. But you can also engage in racial justice practices at the individual level. What organizations, causes, or individuals involved in racial justice can you support through sacrificial giving? What is the most you can contribute rather than putting forth the minimum amount that makes you feel good about yourself?

Be Careful about Referencing Racists

The Puritans were a group of Christians who thought that the Church of England needed to be purified because it was still too similar, in their view, to Roman Catholicism. In the early 1600s, groups of Puritans colonized New England and sought to form communities that embodied their vision of religious orthodoxy. Unfortunately, many of the most prominent Puritans failed to turn their efforts at purifying the church to their own views on Native Americans and people of African descent.

In 2012, spoken word artist Jason "Propaganda" Petty released "Precious Puritans." In this poem, he called out pastors who uncritically cited religious leaders who advocated race-based chattel slavery and practiced discrimination toward racial and ethnic minorities.

> Would you quote Columbus to Cherokees?
> Would you quote Cortez to Aztecs, even if they
>   theology was good?
> It just sings a blind privilege, wouldn't you agree?
> Your precious Puritans.[7]

Too many leaders who reference these Puritans, deemed "precious" because of their theological contributions, completely ignore or devalue the impact of such an action on racial and ethnic minorities. How can a person of color, or even another white person, look to racists as moral exemplars and models of virtue?

> Hey, Pastor, you know it's hard for me when you
>   quote Puritans.
> Oh, the precious Puritans.
> Have you not noticed our facial expressions?
> One of bewilderment, and heartbreak, like "Not you
>   too, Pastor"[8]

It is one matter to quote people with racist views—whether in churches, classrooms, in the home or elsewhere—for historical and education purposes. It is another matter to hold them up as people worthy of imitating to the very groups they would have considered less than human. It is crushing for leaders to blithely quote and promote racists such as Robert E. Lee, Jonathan Edwards, George Whitefield, and R. L. Dabney without considering, or even knowing they need to consider, the impact of their racial views and actions. So be careful if you quote racists. Perfection cannot be the standard for learning from someone. If that were the case, we could not learn from anyone except Jesus. Everyone has made mistakes. But the point is not to cover over these failings as if they did not occur. Nor should we cling to white supremacists as examples of moral or civic virtue. Don't overlook the racism of the people you might reference.

To some extent, teaching about racists is unavoidable. If you want to talk about the political foundations of the United States, you have to talk about George Washington, a man who owned slaves. If you want to discuss the expansion of the Christian church in various parts of the world, you have to talk about the oppression of indigenous peoples in the name of God.

All of this should be put into context. We cannot change the record of leaders and historical figures who held abhorrent racial views. What we can do is make sure these parts of their record are known just as much as the other parts. We can discuss the impact of their actions on people who held less power, had less money, and were part of groups considered minorities, subhuman, or "other."

Too many people avoid talking about the shameful racial history of individuals or institutions out of a desire to dodge conflict or swerve around uncomfortable conversations. But when a person, particularly a member of a racial or ethnic minority, later discovers that racist history, there is a feeling of betrayal and hurt. It is better to take on the topic directly and work through the complexities of learning from flawed people than to pretend as if they were perfect.

Of course, one productive way to move beyond this conundrum is not to cite such racists at all. While there is value in learning about people who held racist views because of their historical importance, there is no imperative to hold up such people as positive examples. There may be other people—not perfect but admirable—who would be more helpful to cite. Instead of exerting incredible efforts to redeem the reputation of racists, research and share about the people who fought racism and other forms of injustice. Committing to finding people who did not think owning, segregating, or oppressing people because of their racial or ethnic background is a valuable racial justice practice. It expands our repertoire of people to learn from beyond our simplistic historical narratives. We should be careful about putting anyone on a pedestal, but surely there are better people to emulate than unrepentant racists.

Refuse to Platform Racists

Hoschton, Georgia, is a small town of about 2,000 people forty-five-minutes northwest of Atlanta. The town catapulted onto national headlines in 2019 when the city's mayor and a city councilman, both white, made racist remarks. In reviewing candidates for the city administrator position, mayor Theresa Kenerly removed Keith Henry, a Black man, from consideration because she allegedly said, "He is black, and the city isn't ready for this."[9] To add to the controversy, city councilman Jim Cleveland expressed his views against interracial marriage a short time later. In an unprompted comment during an interview, he said, "I'm a Christian and my Christian beliefs are you don't do interracial marriage. That's the way I was brought up and that's the way I believe."[10]

People in Hoschton were understandably upset by the actions and words of their local leaders. They initiated a recall election, but both Kenerly and Cleveland resigned before it took place. The two city legislators' racist views and comments resulted in losing the privilege of elected office and leading their neighbors.

People who make blatantly racist comments or commit racist deeds and refuse to change should lose the privilege of their platform. What will your response be when a popular personality engages in racism? Will you continue to reference their work? Will you promote their books and articles? Will you cite them in sermons, presentations, or speeches? If you do, what does it communicate about how serious you think racism is?

A common word for deplatforming someone or refusing to promote their brand or work is "cancelling." Many people decry "cancel culture" as the petulant response of overly sensitive people or as the overzealous response of those for whom political correctness is all-important. Some Christians retort, "Jesus never cancelled me, so I won't cancel anyone." Social media certainly makes it easy to pile on someone for their mistakes. From a racial justice perspective, though, deplatforming or cancelling does not refer to the person's very being. It concerns only their work and their influence. If someone openly traffics in racism, then they should not be given the privilege of a large audience or influence. Deplatforming should always make room for change and growth. Everyone deserves a chance to learn and repent. But until that happens, we should consider refusing to platform people who act in racist ways.

What does it look like to refuse to platform racists? On social media, refuse to retweet or repost them. If they have products for sale, refuse to buy them. If they are speaking at a conference, contact the organizers and bring the issue to their attention. If they refuse to make a change in the lineup, consider not going. Use the money you would have spent on the conference or event to support a minority-led organization. The point is to discourage racist behavior by using your choice as a consumer or supporter to create the constructive pressure to change.

Use Your Platform Productively

Colin Kaepernick broke records running and throwing as a quarterback at the University of Nevada, and then he broke football by taking a knee during the national anthem. During the 2016 National Football League season, the 49ers signal-caller knelt during the national anthem to protest against racism and, specifically, anti-Black police brutality. His gesture sparked an ongoing controversy. Some supported his stance as a public witness against injustice. Others condemned him for disrespecting the flag, the nation, and the armed forces. President Trump said in an interview, "Frankly the NFL should have suspended him for one game, and he would have never done it again. . . . But I will tell you, you cannot disrespect our country, our flag, our anthem—you cannot do that."[11]

The consequences for Kaepernick's "stand" against racism were far more severe than a one-game suspension. The quarterback who once led his team to the Super Bowl has not played for an NFL team since early 2017. Kaepernick formally filed a claim against the NFL for colluding to keep him off of teams because of his political stances. He withdrew the claim in 2019 in exchange for an undisclosed amount. Kaepernick has continued and expanded his racial justice work, namely through charitable giving and his Know Your Rights Camp, which advances "the liberation and well-being of Black and Brown communities" through education.[12]

Kaepernick stands in a line of athletes—from Muhammad Ali to Serena Williams—who used their prominence as celebrities to advance the cause of racial justice. Their courage in the face of racism sometimes cost them their jobs in the prime of their careers. Yet they are exemplars of what it looks like to use and risk one's platform in order to fight racism.

Very few people attain the status of becoming a professional athlete, but you don't have to be an elite athlete or have hundreds of thousands of followers on social media to have a platform and to use it for good. Everyone has influence. Some have more than others, but each person can make an impact for racial justice.

How do you know it is time to use your platform for racial justice? Here are four times to do so. First, use your platform if the issue directly affects your community. If an unarmed person of color is brutalized or killed by law enforcement in your city, if an immigrant population in your community is being discriminated against, or if someone in your faith community is experiencing the adverse effects of racism, then your voice is vital to making sure people know what you believe and with whom you stand.

Second, if a prominent official or leader makes racist comments, it may be time to raise your voice. People with large platforms engage in racist actions way too frequently. Since they have large audiences, they can create narratives that lead to prejudice and even violence. When this is the case, your words and actions can help create a counternarrative that promotes racial justice.

Third, if someone from your ideological, political, or religious group is harming the cause of racial justice, consider making a public statement. While we cannot account for the actions of everyone with whom we share some affiliation, we can make it clear that others within that same group hold different views and want to fight racism.

Fourth, use your platform for racial justice when an issue or incident grips you and won't let go. We are all affected in different ways by different events. What pierces your heart may be unknown to others, and it is up to you to bring attention to the injustice. Follow your conscience, shaped by a justice-loving community, and speak and act in solidarity with the oppressed.

Here are a few steps to help you understand your personal influence and use it to promote racial justice. First, determine your platform. It may not be large—it could be your immediate family, your workplace, or your faith community—but everyone has a sphere of influence. Those with bigger platforms have a more conspicuous voice, and their voices are more conspicuously absent when they do not speak up about racial justice. This is not just for white people. People of color have platforms they should employ for racial justice as well. Since people of color have to deal with racism every day in numerous ways, their responsibility is different, and they should take their mental and emotional capacity into account before sharing.

Second, be public about it. A platform is public by nature, so positively using your platform necessitates taking a public stance. This is not about private conversations or behind-the-scenes efforts. Using your platform for the cause of racial justice means people know where you stand because you have broadcast it in some way. This is not about virtue-signaling and saying, "Look at what a good person I am!" It is about being willing to risk your platform, your influence, your reputation for the sake of racial justice.

Third, when you take this stance, do your due diligence to make sure you are saying the right things in the right way. When Colin Kaepernick decided to protest during the anthem, he discussed the ideas with trusted colleagues, including a military veteran, and spent time learning about the issues.[13] Build your awareness of racial justice and develop vital relationships with people from different backgrounds as ways to prepare for using your platform for racial justice.

Finally, prepare for the reaction. There will be those who question why "you're making this about race." Others will want to argue endlessly about a particular turn of phrase or one part of your actions rather than attending to the general thrust of what you're trying to say. Some will disavow you and refuse to listen to your music, read your posts, follow you on social media, or perhaps even talk to you because of your stance for racial justice. But you should be prepared for positive reactions too. The benefit of using your platform for racial justice is that people of color feel seen and heard. White people can be challenged in a good way and can rethink their assumptions. But no matter the reaction or the ratio of positive to negative responses, using your platform to promote racial justice is simply the right thing to do.

Support Minority-Owned or -Led Businesses

We have numerous opportunities to demonstrate commitment to racial justice through the ways we spend money and which businesses we patronize or forego. The next time your business, club, or church has an event, intentionally choose to have a minority-owned or -led business cater the function. If you need music, consider people of color for the artists. If you need to commission a logo or a t-shirt design, use a graphic design service from a person of color. If you need plumbing, accounting, or legal services, seek out people of color to financially support their business. You may even consider paying slightly more in the form of a tip or a bonus to offset the financial impediments that many people of color face when running their own business.

Take Your Talents to Minority-Owned or -Led Organizations

Howard University, a historically Black College or University (HBCU), had a basketball team that had not been to the NCAA tournament in thirty years and that won just four games in the 2019 season. Yet in the summer of 2020, they scored a huge win when five-star recruit Makur Maker committed to the Bison. The seven-foot-tall star explained his decision on Twitter, "I need to make the HBCU movement real so that others will follow."[14]

Maker had his pick of elite basketball programs at predominantly white universities, but he chose to take his talents to an HBCU in order to be in an environment supportive of racial and ethnic minorities and to bring attention to colleges and universities that have played a pivotal role in the Black community for decades. Black people and other people of color may need to follow Maker's example by taking their skills, talents, and expertise to minority-owned or -led organizations.

Racial and ethnic minorities should consider the difficulties that many minority-owned or -led organizations have in recruiting top-tier talent and securing financial resources for their mission. If more people of color chose to attend school or work for these institutions it could breathe new life into their work. Whether you write, preach, fundraise, or design, what would happen if you committed to supporting other people of color? This is a costly decision. You will likely make less money, work in more obscurity, and receive criticism for your decision. But you also lend your time and energy to organizations and causes that need you. You could be part of a movement that transforms the landscape of your field so that minority-owned or -led organizations become the first choice for people instead of a last resort.

Support Candidates Committed to Racial Justice—Or Run Yourself

Throughout this book, we have looked at the ways political power has been used and misused in relation to racial justice. Orienting your life toward racial justice must entail ongoing involvement at the policy level. While you may never actually run for elected office yourself, all political campaigns, from the local to the largest national effort, depend on volunteers for success. You can volunteer to knock on doors, make phone calls, or contribute specific skills such as accounting or legal expertise to a campaign. Do you write? Consider composing an op-ed for your local newspaper supporting a particular policy or political candidate. Donating money remains one of the most concrete and important ways to support a political campaign that you believe stands for positive change.

You have probably seen the quote "Be the change you wish to see in the world." It is on bumper stickers, signs, and coffee mugs. It is kitschy and cliché, and it is probably not what Gandhi actually said. His original quote is even more helpful: "If we could change ourselves, the tendencies in the world would also change. As a man changes his own nature, so does the attitude of the world change towards him. . . . We need not wait to see what others do."[15] Too often in racial justice work, we focus on criticism and calling out. For some this seems to be a full-time vocation. At some point, however, we need to get involved in making the changes we say need to happen.

Some people committed to fighting racism may need to consider running for elected office. By holding an elected office you become someone who helps craft the laws that shape our racial reality. While many initially think of national offices in Congress, the opportunities for public policy work are immense, especially at the local level—from school board to city council, from district attorney to county commissioner, from sheriff to judge, from state representative to city clerk. Which office you run for depends on your expertise, your interests, and the kind of support you think you can generate.

Running for office is a massive undertaking and should not be taken on cavalierly. It will cost you time, money, and energy to run a campaign, and that's just the beginning. If you win, then much more work and criticism are coming your way. Many resources exist to help you get started, depending on your state and political leanings. Consult with experts and advisers. Listen to your potential constituents to form a platform. Seek input from people with fundraising and campaign managing experience.

Running for office may sound controversial to those who think people of faith should stay out of politics, but most people at the national level claim some kind of religious tradition. In the 116th Congress, 53.7 percent of the House of Representatives is Protestant Christian, 32.5 percent are Catholic, 6 percent are Jewish, with Hindus, Muslims, Buddhists, and others represented as well. Of US Senators, 60 percent identify as Protestant, 22 percent are Catholic, 4 percent are Mormon, with Judaism and Buddhism among others represented as well.[16] According to the statistics, in fact, religion is overrepresented among elected officials at the national level compared to the general population.

Of course, there are important considerations besides the logistics of running for office if you are a person of faith. Should pastors, imams, rabbis, and other religious leaders run for elected office? As people who represent communities with varying political views, formally affiliating with a political party in an elected position may alienate some members of their religious flock and impede their ability to lead. It may also be difficult to persuade new people to join the religious community if the leader is seen as someone who supports an opposing political party or point of view. Although being an elected official as a religious person can pose unique challenges, there is still a general need (which, of course, includes those without any formal religious affiliation) for people of conviction and high moral standards to run for office.

Reconsider Where You Send Your Kids to School

Nikole Hannah-Jones practices what she preaches. She lives in the Bedford-Stuyvesant neighborhood of New York City. The public schools there routinely score poorly on state standardized evaluations. The student population of these schools is almost entirely comprised of Black and Latino children who are low-income. As such, few of the middle-class residents of the neighborhood send their children to the local public schools.

Hannah-Jones and her husband could have followed the crowd and sent their child to a predominantly white and better resourced school. The choice had profound implications, not just for her as a parent, but for her work as an investigative reporter researching racial segregation in public schools. Housing discrimination, policies around school-funding, and outright racism had all contributed to the segregated state of public schooling. Thus systemic change was necessary. But Hannah-Jones also believed that parents' choices about where to send their kids to school could uphold the existing system or oppose it. "One family, or even a few families, cannot transform a segregated school, but if none of us were willing to go into them, nothing would change," she said.[17] Hannah-Jones and her husband decided to enroll their daughter in a local public school because only by racially and economically integrating public schools would the racist status quo change.

Even though we have to pursue more equitable funding for public schools, the problem is not just an issue of money. It is a matter of pursuing the common good and making sure schools work for all children, not just your own. According to Hannah-Jones, "True integration, true equality, requires a surrendering of advantage, and when it comes to our own children, that can feel almost unnatural."[18]

Every parent of school-age children must face the choice of where to send their children to school and what that means for racial segregation in schools. Schools that are wealthier and white get more resources. Racially and economically integrating public schools would ensure that middle- and upper-class parents would bring their resources and attention to improving the schools their children attend. As long as people who can afford the financial and cultural costs of segregation choose to send their children to separate schools, vast inequality will remain in the system.

Parents must seriously consider the value of racial integration in comparison with better material offerings at other schools. It would indeed be a sacrifice to send your child to a school with fewer resources, but it is a choice that many parents have no choice but to make. It may be that your racial justice journey includes taking the bold step of sending your children to a less prestigious school in order to help write a new story about integration and achievement in our public schools.

Ensure Local Schools Practice Racial Justice

Regardless of where you send your kids to school or even if you have kids at all, you can ensure that your local schools are building racial justice into their curriculum. A relative once asked me for help leading up to a meeting she was having with administrators at her Black child's predominantly white school. She wondered what questions she should ask, and I sent her the following list that you might want to ask of your local schools:

- How and where does the curriculum specifically address Black history, Native American history, and the histories of other people of color?
- What training do teachers receive on culturally responsive teaching and working with racial and ethnic minority students and families?

- Are there written protocols and guidelines for addressing hate speech and racist incidents (including cyberbullying) at the school?
- What is the racial/ethnic composition of the school board, faculty, staff, support staff (i.e., anyone on the payroll)?
- What is the retention rate/tenure of racial and ethnic minority faculty and staff compared to their white peers? How do wages, salaries, and bonuses compare?
- Have you considered hiring racial and ethnic minorities in clusters instead of one or two at a time?
- Do you track academic data by racial and ethnic demographics? How are Black students and students of color doing in relation to white students?
- Do you track discipline, suspensions, and expulsions by race and ethnicity? How do those data compare across demographics?
- Have you had focus groups where parents and guardians of color get a chance to speak into school practices and climate?
- What have you learned from other schools or institutions about racial justice best practices?
- Have you considered forming a standing committee on racial awareness and responsiveness so you can be proactive about racial justice and not always reactive?

These questions in modified form can be asked of any club, sports team, nonprofit, or other organization to ensure they are practicing racial justice.

Orienting your life toward racial justice requires constant reflection and action. It is not a one-time decision. In community with others who share the same concerns, we need to constantly ponder our practices to refine our approach to fighting racism. The ARC of Racial Justice reminds us that we need constantly to commit to changing racist policies. We all have the responsibility daily to decide to take another step on the journey toward racial justice.

CONCLUSION

I began this book by introducing you to Fannie Lou Hamer and offering a glimpse into her life of activism. Hamer is a model of what it means to be a faith-filled fighter for racial justice. She dedicated years of her life to pursuing equity and dignity for Black people and the poor, and her Christian faith was not incidental to her activism but integral to it. She once said, "That's why I love the song, 'This Little Light of Mine.' . . . I don't mind my light shining; I don't hide that I'm fighting for freedom because Christ died to set us free."[1] Her courage in the face of white supremacy should inspire us all to confront—rather than compromise with—racism.

In March of 1977, doctors admitted Fannie Lou to Mound Bayou Community Hospital, staffed entirely by Black people when it was founded in 1942, for a combination of issues arising from diabetes, cancer, and heart disease.[2] June Johnson, a close friend, was one of the last people to see her alive. "She stated she was so tired, she wanted all of us to remember her and to keep up the work," Johnson recalled.[3]

Yet for all of Fannie Lou Hamer's labors, can we say she succeeded? Was she effective in her struggle for freedom? We have seen that her twin passions of securing voting rights for the disenfranchised and alleviating poverty have still not been realized. In her life she gained the respect of many, but on her deathbed she had few people around her and even less money to help ease her discomfort. An associate, Owen Brooks, had to raise the money to pay for her funeral.[4]

The value of fighting racism cannot be gauged simply by looking at the number of laws passed or individuals elected. It cannot be measured in funds raised or in how many members an organization has. These data points matter, but they are not all that matter. Fighting racism is not just about how it changes the world; it's also about how it changes you.

When I began intentionally dedicating my time, expertise, and energy to fighting racism, my life did not become easier. In many ways it became harder. I opened myself up to arguments and attacks. Relationships became strained and some were broken. In paying closer attention to racial injustice and feeling the pain of it more acutely, I became in some ways like the "man of sorrows" the prophet Isaiah describes (Isa. 53:3 ESV).

But the travails of this journey of racial justice have brought me a deeper sense of three realities: God's presence, the community of co-laborers, and my identity. Fannie Lou Hamer said that when she got involved in the struggle for freedom she understood God's presence better and felt God's nearness and sustaining strength more clearly. "It's a funny thing since I started working for Christ—it's kind of like the twenty-third of Psalms when he says, 'Thou prepareth a table before me in the presence of mine enemies. Thou anointed my head with oil and my cup runneth over.'"[5] As difficult as Hamer's life had been before the day she attempted to register for the first time, it got exponentially more difficult thereafter. People shot at her house, officers beat her in a Mississippi jail, and she faced exhaustion crisscrossing the country for civil rights. God did not make her life easier when she publicly took on the cause of racial justice, but God did make himself known.

I think I have grown in my understanding of this principle as well. In the times when I have felt most burdened by the bigotry of this world, Christ has come alongside to make the yoke easy and the burden light (cf. Matt. 11:30). Although the fight for racial justice has alienated me from some, it has brought me into community with many others. I started what became The Witness, a Black Christian Collective, late one night sitting alone at my dining room table. Nearly a decade later we have a team of people who have become like family and with whom I work shoulder to shoulder in this effort for equality. My church now includes not just the people in my local congregation but the community of people across the country and even on different continents striving to love God and neighbor. The camaraderie and allyship I have felt on this journey can only be experienced from within the struggle for justice.

Fighting for racial justice has taught me more about . . . me. I am far more fragile than I like to admit. I am subject to the same preconceived notions and judgmentalism that I decry in others. I get tired, frustrated, angry. I have also discovered reservoirs of previously untapped resilience. I am learning to ask for help when I need it. I have gleaned lessons from others about how to long for justice and still have joy at the same time.

This can all be true for you too.

To the trepidatious, those who worry about what taking bolder steps down this journey of racial justice might cost them, know this: the only way to grow is to go. The only way to increase your courage, perseverance, and skill is to get started. You will never be able to prepackage these characteristics. They are only gained by doing. So get started. The steps do not have to be large, but if you keep going, baby steps turn into long strides toward freedom. And let me take the pressure off. You will make mistakes. You will stumble and perhaps fall at times. But failure is not in the fall but in whether you stay down.

To those intrepid travelers who have already been trudging along the way for years, know this: you are already effective. You may have particular goals and metrics that have not been met, and that can be discouraging. But you have already succeeded because you got started. Think back through the history of this nation. How many people chose compromise and complicity rather than taking up the cause of racial justice?

How many people let others do all the work while they sat safely in their silence? You are one of the few who chose to take on the risks of fighting racism, and in that decision you have already achieved a victory.

We cannot give up. We are people of hope. Hope is not blind optimism. It is a realistic assessment of current conditions with the faith that tomorrow can be different. We are people who believe that a brutal, unjustified murder resulted in a resurrection. We believe that a poor carpenter from Nazareth conquered death and is forming a people who will join in this triumph. Each day that we live is the opportunity to be witnesses to the resurrection life and the coming of the kingdom of God. We pray and work for that kingdom to come and for God's will to be done, not just in the sweet by and by, but right here and now. The journey for racial justice continues, but the music we hear along the way is not a funeral dirge; it is festival music leading us to a banquet of blessings and a harvest of righteousness. Today is the day and now is the time to join this journey toward racial justice.

NOTES

Chapter 1: How to Fight Racism

1. Evan Hill, Ainara Tiefenthäler, Christiaan Triebert, Drew Jordan, Haley Willis, and Robin Stein, "How George Floyd Was Killed in Police Custody," *New York Times*, May 31, 2020, https://www.nytimes.com/2020/05/31/us/george-floyd-investigation.html.
2. Christina Carrega and Sabina Ghebremedhin, "Timeline: inside the Investigation of Breonna Taylor's Killing and Its Aftermath," ABC News, June 20, 2020, https://abcnews.go.com/US/timeline-inside-investigation-breonna-taylors-killing-aftermath/story?id=71217247.
3. Jennifer Rae Taylor and Kayla Vinson, "Ahmaud Arbery and the Local Legacy of Lynching," Marshall Project, May 21, 2020, https://www.themarshallproject.org/2020/05/21/ahmaud-arbery-and-the-local-legacy-of-lynching.
4. Troy Closson, "Amy Cooper's 911 Call, and What's Happened Since," *New York Times*, July 8, 2020. https://www.nytimes.com/2020/07/08/nyregion/amy-cooper-false-report-charge.html.
5. Enjoli Francis and Mary Booth, "New Police Documents Reveal Deadly Minutes Inside South Carolina Church," ABC News, October 29, 2015, https://abcnews.go.com/US/police-documents-reveal-deadly-minutes-inside-south-carolina/story?id=34836336.
6. Andrew Katz, "Unrest in Virginia," *Time*, https://time.com/charlottesville-white-nationalist-rally-clashes/.
7. "Trump's Racism: An Oral History," *Atlantic*, June 2019, https://www.theatlantic.com/magazine/archive/2019/06/trump-racism-comments/588067/.
8. Yelena Dzhanova, "Here's a Running List of All the Big Companies Observing Juneteenth This Year," *CNBC*, June 17,

2020, https://www.cnbc.com/2020/06/17/here-are-the-companies
-observing-juneteenth-this-year.html#:~:text=Computer%20
software%20company%20Adobe%20announced,slavery%20in%20
the%20United%20States.

9. Kenya Evelyn, "Black US Authors Top *New York Times* Bestseller
   List as Protests Continue," *The Guardian*, June 11, 2020, https://
   www.theguardian.com/books/2020/jun/11/new-york-times-best
   seller-list-black-authors.

10. Martin L. King Jr., "I Have a Dream," speech. Lincoln Memorial,
    Washington, DC, August 28, 1963.

11. This definition is cited in Beverly Daniel Tatum, *Why Are All
    the Black Kids Sitting Together in the Cafeteria? And Other
    Conversations about Race* (New York: Basic, 1997). More about
    the definition of racism will be explained in chapter 3.

12. See "What's the Difference between 'Equity' and 'Equality'?,"
    Lakeshore Ethnic Diversity Alliance, https://ethnicdiversity.org
    /equity-vs-equality/.

13. Willie James Jennings, *The Christian Imagination: Theology and
    the Origins of Race* (New Haven, CT: Yale University Press, 2010), 8.

14. This was the image of Jesus popularized by Warner Sallman's
    painting "Head of Christ" (1940). For more about visual
    representations of Jesus, see Edward J. Blum and Paul Harvey,
    *The Color of Christ The Son of God and the Saga of Race in
    America* (Chapel Hill: University of North Carolina Press, 2012).

15. See Mark Noll, *The Civil War as a Theological Crisis* (Chapel
    Hill: University of North Carolina Press, 2006); and Charles
    Marsh, *God's Long Summer: Stories of Faith and Civil Rights*
    (Princeton, NJ: Princeton University Press, 1997).

16. I write at length about white Christian failings when it comes to
    race in *The Color of Compromise: The Truth about the American
    Church's Complicity in Racism* (Grand Rapids: Zondervan, 2019).

17. Soong-Chan Rah, *Many Colors: Cultural Intelligence for a
    Changing Church* (Chicago: Moody Publishers, 2010), 56.

18. Martin Luther King Jr., "Letter from Birmingham Jail," April 16,
    1963.

19. Walter Brueggemann, *The Prophetic Imagination*, 40th anniv. ed.
    (Minneapolis: Fortress, 2018), 129.

20. Bryan Stevenson, "This Is the Conversation about Race that We
    Need to Have Now," Ideas.Ted.com, August 17, 2017, https://ideas

.ted.com/opinion-this-is-the-conversation-about-race-that-we-need
-to-have-now/.

21. W. E. B. DuBois, *John Brown: A Biography; A New Edition with Primary Documents by John David Smith* (New York: Sharpe, 1997), 33.

22. Chana Kai Lee, *For Freedom's Sake: The Life of Fannie Lou Hamer* (Urbana: University of Illinois Press, 1997), 25.

23. For more information on the life of Fannie Lou Hamer, see Marsh, *God's Long Summer*, ch. 1; Kay Mills, *This Little Light of Mine: The Life of Fannie Lou Hamer* (Lexington: University Press of Kentucky, 2007); Maegan Parker Brooks, *Fannie Lou Hamer: America's Freedom Fighting Woman* (Lanham, MD: Rowman & Littlefield, 2020).

24. Charles McLaurin, "Voice of Calm," *Sojourners Magazine*, December 11, 1982, as cited in Marsh, *God's Long Summer*, 24.

Chapter 2: How to Explain Race and the Image of God

1. "Calls Rhinelander Dupe of Girl He Wed," *New York Times*, November 10, 1929, pp. 1, 8.

2. Theodore Johnson III, "When One Of New York's Glitterati Married A 'Quadroon,'" NPR, June 7, 2014, https://www.npr.org /sections/codeswitch/2014/06/07/319813854/when-one-of-new -yorks-glitterati-married-a-quadroon.

3. Racial justice advocates usually avoid the term *nonwhite* because it describes people based on what they are *not* rather than what they are. Further it defines all people in relation to whiteness and white people instead of identifying people groups as having an independent existence in and of themselves.

4. Lydia Ramsey Pflanzer and Samantha Lee, "Our DNA Is 99.9% the Same as the Person Next to Us—and We're Surprisingly Similar to a Lot of Other Living Things," *Business Insider*, April 3, 2018, https://www.businessinsider.com/comparing-genetic -similarity-between-humans-and-other-things-2016–5.

5. For more on the mutability of race see Nell Irvin Painter, *The History of White People* (New York: Norton, 2010); David R. Roediger, *Working Toward Whiteness: How Immigrants Became White, The Strange Journey from Ellis Island to the Suburbs* (New York: Basic, 2006); Noel Ignatiev, *How the Irish Became White* (New York: Routledge, 1995).

6. Samantha Cooney, "Michelle Obama Reveals the Most Difficult Part of Her Time as First Lady," *Time*, July 26, 2017, https://time .com/4874387/michelle-obama-first-lady-racism/.

7. Mandalit del Barco, "How Kodak's Shirley Cards Set Photography's Skin Tone Standards," *Morning Edition*, NPR, November 13, 2014, https://www.npr.org/2014/11/13/363517842/for-decades-kodak-s -shirley-cards-set-photography-s-skin-tone-standard.

8. Also see Genesis 6:5, 7; Psalm 12:1, 8; Ecclesiastes 3:10.

9. J. Daniel Hays, *From Every People and Nation: A Biblical Theology of Race* (Downers Grove, IL: InterVarsity Press, 2003), 28–30.

10. Taylor Branch, *At Canaan's Edge: America in the King Years, 1965–1968* (New York: Simon & Schuster, 2006), 684–85.

11. Branch, *At Canaan's Edge*, 731.

12. Peniel Joseph, *Waiting 'Til the Midnight Hour: A Narrative History of Black Power in America* (New York: Holt, 2006), 197.

13. Clayborn Carson, "Jesse Jackson," *The Reader's Companion to American History* (Houghton Mifflin), https://web.archive.org/web /20040203015206/http://college.hmco.com/history/readerscomp /rcah/html/ah_046500_jacksonjesse.htm.

14. Elizabeth Day, "#BlackLivesMatter: The Birth of a New Civil Rights Movement," *Guardian*, July 19, 2015, https://www.theguardian.com/ world/2015/jul/19/blacklivesmatter-birth-civil-rights-movement.

15. D. A. Horton, *Intensional: Kingdom Ethnicity in a Divided World* (Colorado Springs, CO: NavPress, 2019), 39.

16. A point that public theologian Ekemini Uwan makes clear in her article, "Idolatry and the Image of God," *Reformed Margins*, January 24, 2017, https://reformedmargins.com/3489-2/.

17. Herman Bavinck, *Reformed Dogmatics*, vol. 2, *God and Creation*, ed. John Bolt (Grand Rapids: Baker Academic, 2004), 555.

18. Charles Carroll, *"The Negro a Beast"; or, "In the Image of God"* (St. Louis: American Book and Bible Society, 1900), 90, https:// archive.org/stream/thenegrobeastori00carrrich/thenegrobeastori 00carrrich_djvu.txt.

19. Carroll, *"The Negro a Beast"*, 7.

20. Jordan Valinsky. "The Aunt Jemima Brand, Acknowledging Its Racist Past, Will Be Retired," CNN, June 17, 2020, https://www .cnn.com/2020/06/17/business/aunt-jemima-logo-change/index.html.

21. Of course the same challenge could be applied to issues of sexism. Think of women theologians who have influenced you. If only

men have shaped your theology, then you are missing wisdom from half of God's image bearers.

22. Howard Thurman, *Jesus and the Disinherited* (Boston: Beacon, 1996), 13.

23. James Cone, *Black Theology and Black Power* (1969; Maryknoll: Orbis, 1997), xxv.

24. Baptist Press (@baptistpress), "The EC has voted, on behalf of the SBC, to withdraw fellowship from Raleigh White Baptist Church in Albany, Ga., based on 'clear evidence' of racial discrimination. #sbcam18," Twitter, June 11, 2018, https://twitter .com/baptistpress/status/1006203896052830208?s=20.

25. Erin B. Logan, "An All-White Church Intended to Give Its Building to a Black Congregation. The Plan Fell Apart," *Washington Post*, June 14, 2018, https://www.washingtonpost.com /news/acts-of-faith/wp/2018/06/13/an-all-white-church-planned-to -give-its-building-to-a-black-congregation-instead-they-clashed/.

26. Logan, "An All-White Church Intended."

Chapter 3: How to Explore Your Racial Identity

1. Christine Hauser, "'Fees Must Fall': Anatomy of the Student Protests in South Africa," *New York Times*, September 22, 2016, https://www.nytimes.com/2016/09/23/world/africa/fees-must-fall -anatomy-of-the-student-protests-in-south-africa.html.

2. Mookgo S. Kgatle, "The Role of the Church in the #FeesMustFall Movement in South Africa: Practical Theological Reflection," *HTS Theological Studies* 74, no. 1 (2018): 2.

3. Ra'eesa Pather, "Protest, Politics and Prayers at South Africa's Universities," *Mail & Guardian*, February 25, 2016, https://mg.co .za/article/2016–02–25-protest-politics-and-prayers-at-south -africas-universities/.

4. Teboho Maktabane, presentation, Ubukho Bakhe Church, Capetown, South Africa, November 30, 2019.

5. Maktabane, 2019.

6. Maktabane, 2019.

7. Beverly Daniel Tatum, *Why Are All the Black Kids Sitting Together in the Cafeteria, and Other Conversations about Race* (New York: Basic, 2017), 77.

8. William E. Cross called the process of racial identity development among Black people "nigrescence," a French word that means

"the process of becoming black." He later updated his theories in *Shades of Black: Diversity in African American Identity* (Philadelphia: Temple University Press, 1991).

9. Cross, *Shades of Black*, 95–96. Due to the interconnectedness of race, ethnicity, and culture, Tatum uses the expanded term, "racial-ethnic-cultural" identity (REC) as well, but the stages of development remain essentially the same.

10. "Inside the Tunnel," Multicultural Student Services, Boise State University, https://www.boisestate.edu/mss/tunnel-of-oppression/inside-the-tunnel/.

11. The notes of the original table read as follow: "This model does not suggest that all persons proceed through all stages; rather, it outlines the steps and eventual outcomes of full identity development for those who engage the issues and pursue the process (especially during the college years.). Neither Cross nor Tatum define or distinguish between ethnic and racialized identity. Nor do they use the terminology 'people of color,' 'co-ethnics,' or 'racialization' in their presentation of this model."

12. Robin DiAngelo, *White Fragility: Why It's So Hard for White People to Talk about Racism* (Boston: Beacon Press, 2018), 77.

13. Daniel Hill, *White Awake: An Honest Look at What It Means to Be White* (Downers Grove, IL: InterVarsity Press, 2017), 3–4.

14. Don Gonyea, "Majority Of White Americans Say They Believe Whites Face Discrimination," NPR, October 24, 2017, https://www.npr.org/2017/10/24/559604836/majority-of-white-americans-think-theyre-discriminated-against.

15. Renni Eddo-Lodge, *Why I'm No Longer Talking to White People about Race* (New York: Bloomsbury, 2017), 89.

16. "Quick Facts," United States Census Bureau, https://www.census.gov/quickfacts/fact/table/US/PST045218.

17. Joyce Beatty, "Statistics Don't Lie: Corporate America Lacks Minorities, Women," *The Hill*, October 29, 2019, https://thehill.com/blogs/congress-blog/politics/467809-a-wake-up-call-for-corporate-america-statistics-dont-lie.

18. Beatrice Jin, "Congress's Incoming Class Is Younger, Bluer, and More Diverse than Ever," *Politico*, November 23, 2018, https://www.politico.com/interactives/2018/interactive_116th-congress-freshman-younger-bluer-diverse/.

19. "African American Senators," United States Senate (website),

https://www.senate.gov/pagelayout/history/h_multi_sections
_and_teasers/Photo_Exhibit_African_American_Senators.htm.

20. Harriet Jacobs, *Incidents in the Life of a Slave Girl, Written by Herself* (Digireads.com Publishing, 2009).

21. Joan Didion, *Slouching towards Bethlehem* (1968; repr., New York: Farrar, Straus and Giroux, 1990), 139.

22. The Disney film *Zootopia*, for instance, presents ample opportunities to discuss differences, prejudice, and reconciliation in the context of an animated movie that uses different animals in ways analogous to different people groups in the real world.

23. Derald Wing Sue and David Sue, *Counseling the Culturally Diverse: Theory and Practice*, 4th ed. (New York: Wiley, 2003), 50.

24. Juliana Menasce Horowitz, Anna Brown, and Kiana Cox, "Race in America 2019," Pew Research Center, April 9, 2019, https://www.pewsocialtrends.org/2019/04/09/race-in-america-2019/.

25. Gemima St. Louis, "Leveling the Mental Health Counseling Racial Playing Field," *Psychology Today*, February 28, 2018, https://www.psychologytoday.com/us/blog/mind-matters/201802/leveling-the-mental-health-counseling-racial-playing-field.

Chapter 4: How to Study the History of Race

1. James Baldwin, "Unnameable Objects, Unspeakable Crimes," *Blackstate*, August 3, 2016, https://blackstate.com/james-baldwin-unnameable-objects-unspeakable-crimes/.

2. Timothy Edwards, "Ad Fontes: Erasmus and the Bible Translation That Rocked the Christian World," New Saint Andrews College, January 18, 2016, https://www.nsa.edu/ad-fontes-erasmus-bible/.

3. "Civil War at 150: Still Relevant, Still Divisive," Pew Research Center: U.S. Politics and Policy, April 8, 2011, https://www.people-press.org/2011/04/08/civil-war-at-150-still-relevant-still-divisive/.

4. "Confederate States of America—Declaration of the Immediate Causes Which Induce and Justify the Secession of South Carolina from the Federal Union," The Avalon Project: Documents in Law, History, and Diplomacy (Yale Law School: Lillian Goldman Library), https://avalon.law.yale.edu/19th_century/csa_scarsec.asp.

5. "Confederate States of America—Mississippi Secession," The Avalon Project: Documents in Law, History, and Diplomacy (Yale Law School: Lillian Goldman Library), https://avalon.law.yale.edu/19th_century/csa_missec.asp.

6. Thomas E. Schott, *Alexander H. Stephens: A Biography* (Baton Rouge: Louisiana State University Press, 1988), 334.

7. "About" webpage, *Black Perspectives*, https://www.aaihs.org/about-black-perspectives/.

8. Visit https://www.washingtonpost.com/news/made-by-history/.

9. Kevin Gannon, "Objective History Is Impossible. And That's a Fact," *The Tattooed Professor* (blog), May 9, 2016, https://www.thetattooedprof.com/2016/05/09/objective-history-is-impossible-and-thats-a-fact/.

10. Ashplant, T.G. and Adrian Wilson. "Whig History and Present-Centred History," *The Historical Journal*, Vol. 31, No. 1 (Mar., 1988), 3.

11. Mark Charles and Soong-Chan Rah, *Unsettling Truths: The Ongoing Dehumanizing Legacy of the Doctrine of Discovery* (Downers Grove, IL: InterVarsity Press, 2019), 13–14.

12. One tool for learning which Native American nations lived in a certain area is the website: nativeland.ca.

13. Mitch Landrieu, "Mitch Landrieu's Speech on the Removal of Confederate Monuments in New Orleans," speech, *New York Times*, https://www.nytimes.com/2017/05/23/opinion/mitch-landrieus-speech-transcript.html?_r=0.

14. Landrieu, "Speech on the Removal of Confederate Monuments."

15. To find out which statues your state has in the Capital, visit the "Architect of the Capitol" website at https://www.aoc.gov/capitol-hill/national-statuary-hall-collection/nsh-location.

16. Kelsey Davis Petts, "University of Mississippi to Relocate Confederate Monument," *Mississippi Today*, June 18, 2020, https://mississippitoday.org/2020/06/18/universtiy-of-mississippi-to-relocate-confederate-monument/.

17. Putting Confederate statues into museums is not without its difficulties. The cost to remove, transport, and preserve such works is enormous. In addition, the physical size of many of these statues means they would dominate the limited spaces of most museums. For more see an article by Janeen Bryant, Benjamin Filene, Louis Nelson, Jennifer Scott, and Suzanne Seriff, "Are Museums the Right Home for Confederate Monuments?," *Smithsonian Magazine*, May 7, 2018.

18. Hannah Natonson, "There's a New Way to Deal with Confederate Monuments: Signs That Explain Their Racist

History," *Washington Post*, September 22, 2019, https://www
.washingtonpost.com/history/2019/09/22/theres-new-way-deal
-with-confederate-monuments-signs-that-explain-their-racist
-history/.

19. Margaret Walker Alexander (1915–1998) was a Black American
poet, novelist, and professor. She wrote the novel *Jubilee* based
on oral history from her grandmother as well as her own
meticulous historical research. In 1968 she founded the Institute
for the Study of the History, Life, and Culture of Black People at
Jackson State University.

20. Faith Karimi, "The US Loses Two Icons of the Civil Rights
Movement in One Day," CNN, July 18, 2020, https://www.cnn
.com/2020/07/18/us/john-lewis-ct-vivian-dead/index.html.

21. Visit oralhistory.org for extensive resources and training materials
for doing oral history.

22. "Conducting Oral Histories with Family Members: Guidelines
and Tips," PDF. https://www.library.ucla.edu/sites/default/files
/UCLA-COHR_Interviewing-Family-Members.pdf

23. "Universities Studying Slavery (USS): The Birth of a Movement,"
President's Commission on Slavery and the University, University
of Virginia, https://slavery.virginia.edu/universities-studying
-slavery-uss-the-birth-of-a-movement/.

24. "Universities Studying Slavery—The Birth of a Movement."

25. Eric Foner, *Reconstruction: America's Unfinished Revolution,
1863–1877* (New York: Harper & Row, 1988).

26. The National Juneteenth Observance Foundation has been
working to make Juneteenth a federal holiday. See http://www
.nationaljuneteenth.com/.

27. See the website for the 2019 SWLA Juneteenth Music Festival,
https://www.swlajuneteenth.org/juneteenth-music-festival.

28. William Faulkner, *Requiem for a Nun* (repr., New York: Vintage
International, 2011), 73.

Chapter 5: How to Do Reconciliation Right

1. "Filibuster and Cloture," United States Senate, https://www
.senate.gov/artandhistory/history/common/briefing/Filibuster
_Cloture.htm.

2. Roxanne Dunbar-Ortiz, *An Indigenous Peoples' History of the
United States* (Boston: Beacon, 2014), 110.

3. Derrick R. Rosenior, "The Rhetoric of Pentecostal Racial Reconciliation: Looking Back to Move Forward," in *A Liberating Spirit: Pentecostals and Social Action in North America*, ed. Steven M. Studebaker and Michael Wilkinson (Eugene, OR: Pickwick, 2010), 72.

4. "Resolution on Racial Reconciliation on the 150th Anniversary of the Founding of the Southern Baptist Convention," Southern Baptist Convention, Atlanta, GA, 1995, http://www.sbc.net /resolutions/899/resolution-on-racial-reconciliation-on-the-150th -anniversary-of-the-southern-baptist-convention.

5. Gayle White, "Clergy Conference Stirs Historic Show of Unity," *Christianity Today*, April 8, 1996, https://www.christianitytoday .com/ct/1996/april8/6t4088.html.

6. Mariella Savidge, "Local Pastors Join 40,000 at Promise Keepers Event," *The Morning Call*, February 22, 1996, https://www.mcall .com/news/mc-xpm-1996–02–22–3077287-story.html.

7. Savidge, "Local Pastors Join 40,000."

8. Aaron Earls, "America's Churches Are Becoming More Diverse," *Facts and Trends*, June 27, 2018, https://factsandtrends.net/2018 /06/27/americas-churches-are-becoming-more-diverse/.

9. Curtiss Paul DeYoung, Michael O. Emerson, George Yancey, and Karen Chai Kim, *United by Faith: The Multiracial Congregation as an Answer to the Problem of Race* (New York: Oxford University Press, 2003), 171.

10. Chanequa Walker-Barnes, *I Bring the Voices of My People: A Womanist Vision for Racial Reconciliation* (Grand Rapids: Eerdmans, 2019), 12.

11. Walker-Barnes, *I Bring the Voices of My People*, 12.

12. Reggie Ugwu, "Overlooked No More: Robert Johnson, Bluesman Whose Life Was a Riddle," *New York Times*, September 25, 2019, https://www.nytimes.com/2019/09/25/obituaries/robert-johnson -overlooked.html.

13. "Our History," First Presbyterian Church, Augusta, https://first presaugusta.org/about-us/history/.

14. "First Presbyterian Church Augusta," National Park Service, https://www.nps.gov/nr/travel/Augusta/firstpresbyterian.html.

15. George Robertson, "We, and Our Fathers, Have Sinned," First Presbyterian Church, June 26, 2015. https://firstpresaugusta.org /resource/we-and-our-fathers-have-sinned-daniel-98/.

16. Drew Pearson, "The Washington Merry-Go Round," *Indiana Gazette*, September 25, 1958, p. 6.
17. Stephen R. Haynes, *The Last Segregated Hour* (New York: Oxford University Press, 2012), loc. 4655, Kindle.
18. Haynes, *The Last Segregated Hour*, loc. 4984.
19. Haynes, *The Last Segregated Hour*, loc. 4940.
20. Martin Luther King Jr., "Letter from a Birmingham Jail," Birmingham, AL, April 16, 1963.
21. Frank A. Thomas, *How to Preach a Dangerous Sermon* (Nashville: Abingdon, 2018), 86.
22. "Yanez Audio, Squad 151," audio transcript, July 6, 2016, https:// www.ramseycounty.us/sites/default/files/County%20Attorney /Exhibit%201a%20-%20Traffic%20Stop%20Transcript.pdf.
23. Mitch Smith, "Minnesota Officer Acquitted in Killing of Philando Castile," *New York Times*, June 16, 2017, https://www.nytimes .com/2017/06/16/us/police-shooting-trial-philando-castile.html.

Chapter 6: How to Make Friends

1. Thabiti Anyabwile, "The Dos and Don'ts of Racial Harmony," speech, The Gospel Coalition 2015 National Conference, Orlando, FL, April 14, 2015.
2. Anyabwile, "The Dos and Don'ts of Racial Harmony."
3. Tamara C. Johnson, "If You Love Me, Do Your Homework," The Witness, a Black Christian Collective, April 18, 2018, https://the witnessbcc.com/if-you-love-me-do-your-homework/.
4. Emma Frances Bloomfield, "How to Talk to Someone You Believe Is Misinformed about the Coronavirus," *The Conversation*, March 17, 2020, https://theconversation.com/how-to-talk-to-someone-you -believe-is-misinformed-about-the-coronavirus-133044.
5. Bloomfield, "How to Talk to Someone."
6. Bloomfield, "How to Talk to Someone."

Chapter 7: How to Build Diverse Communities

1. "Defining DEI," University of Michigan, https://diversity.umich .edu/about/defining-dei/.
2. Andre Henry, "Black Christians Deserve Better than Companies (and Churches) like Relevant Media Group," *Medium*, September 18, 2019, https://medium.com/@andrehenry/black-christians-deserve -better-than-companies-like-relevant-media-group-42aed44528c9.

3. Martin Luther King Jr., *Where Do We Go From Here: Chaos or Community?* (Boston, MA: Beacon, 1967), 95.

4. "José Vs. Joe: Who Gets A Job?," BuzzFeed presents As/Is, August 30, 2014, YouTube video, https://www.youtube.com/watch?v=PR7SG2C7IVU.

5. Marianne Bertrand and Sendhil Mullainathan, "Are Emily and Greg More Employable than Lakisha and Jamal? A Field Experiment on Labor Market Discrimination," *American Economic Review* 94, no. 4 (September 2004): 991–1013.

6. Marissa Iati, "Southern Baptist Convention's Flagship Seminary Details Its Racist, Slave-Owning past in Stark Report," *Washington Post*, December 12, 2018, https://www.washington post.com/religion/2018/12/12/southern-baptist-conventions -flagship-seminary-admits-all-four-its-founders-owned-slaves/.

7. Ira Katznelson. *When Affirmative Action Was White: An Untold History of Racial Inequality in Twentieth-Century America,* New York: W.W. Norton & Co., 2005, 152.

8. Robert Tamasy, "James McKenzie Baird: 1928–2020," *By Faith Online*, February 3, 2020, https://byfaithonline.com/james -mckenzie-baird-1928–2020/.

9. Anthony Bradley, "Context for the PCA's Repenting of Racism," *World*, June 29, 2016, https://world.wng.org/2016/06/context_for _the_pca_s_repenting_of_racism.

10. "PCA African American Ministry," African American Ministries, https://aampca.org/.

11. Juliana Menasce Horowitz, "Americans See Advantages and Challenges in Country's Growing Racial and Ethnic Diversity," Pew Research Center: Social and Demographic Trends, May 8, 2019, https://www.pewsocialtrends.org/2019/05/08/americans -see-advantages-and-challenges-in-countrys-growing-racial-and -ethnic-diversity/.

12. "The Detroit Millennial Survey," Deloitte, January 2014, https:// www2.deloitte.com/content/dam/Deloitte/global/Documents/About -Deloitte/gx-dttl-2014-millennial-survey-report.pdf.

13. Carla Freeman, "The Case for Cluster Hiring to Diversify Your Faculty," *Chronicle of Higher Education*, October 9, 2019, https:// www.chronicle.com/article/The-Case-for-Cluster-Hiring-to/247301.

14. Campbell Robertson, "A Quiet Exodus: Why Black Worshipers Are Leaving White Evangelical Churches," *New York Times*,

March 9, 2018, https://www.nytimes.com/2018/03/09/us/blacks
-evangelical-churches.html.

15. Lawrence Ware, "Why I'm Leaving the Southern Baptist
Convention," *New York Times*, July 17, 2017, https://www.nytimes
.com/2017/07/17/opinion/why-im-leaving-the-southern-baptist
-convention.html.

Chapter 8: How to Work for Racial Justice

1. The term *beloved community* traces back to Josiah Royce (1855–
1916), an American religious philosopher and one of the founders
of the Fellowship of Reconciliation.

2. Martin Luther King Jr., "Facing the Challenge of a New Age,"
speech, First Annual Institute on Nonviolence and Social Change,
December 3, 1956, via the Martin Luther King Jr. Research and
Education Institute at Stanford University, https://kinginstitute.
stanford.edu/king-papers/documents/facing-challenge-new-age
-address-delivered-first-annual-institute-nonviolence.

3. Martin Luther King Jr., *Where Do We Go from Here: Chaos or
Community?* (Boston: Beacon, 1968), 37–38.

4. Mika Edmondson (@mika_edmondson), "You cannot love your
neighbor while supporting or accepting systems that crush,
exploit, and dehumanize them. You cannot love your neighbor
while accepting less for them and their family than you do for
you and your own," Twitter, December 29, 2017, https://twitter
.com/mika_edmondson/status/946970426449825792?s=20.

5. Alice Walker. "Can't Hate Anybody and See God's Face," *New
York Times*, April 29, 1973, https://timesmachine.nytimes.com
/timesmachine/1973/04/29/97135122.pdf?pdf_redirect=true&ip=0.

6. Adelle M. Banks, "Pastor Says $1 Million from Closing Church Aids
Wider 'Fellowship of the Concerned,'" Religion News Service, August
12, 2019, https://religionnews.com/2019/08/12/pastor-says-1-million-
from-closing-church-aids-wider-fellowship-of-the-concerned/.

7. Canter Brown, *Florida's Black Public Officials, 1867–1924*
(Tuscaloosa: University of Alabama Press, 1998), 4.

8. Jake Wittich, "Cook County State's Attorney Candidates Avoid
Attacks at Bridgeport Debate," *Chicago Sun Times*, February
22, 2020, https://chicago.suntimes.com/2020/2/22/21148918/kim
-foxx-bill-conway-debate-progressive-baptist-church-cook-county
-states-attorneys-office.

9. Visit eac.gov for more information on voting at a national and state level.
10. "Revenue Ruling 2007–41," *IRS.* June 18, 2007. https://www.irs .gov/pub/irs-drop/rr-07-41.pdf
11. Daniel Perlstein, "Teaching Freedom: SNCC and the Creation of the Mississippi Freedom Schools," *History of Education Quarterly* 30, no. 3 (Autumn 1990): 297–324.
12. "About Us," Turn Around Agenda, https://www.turnaround agenda.org/.

Chapter 9: How to Fight Systemic Racism

1. "Quick Facts: Ferguson, Missouri," United States Census Bureau, https://www.census.gov/quickfacts/fergusoncitymissouri.
2. Richard Rothstein, *The Color of Law: A Forgotten History of How Our Government Segregated America* (New York: Liveright, 2017), loc. 884, Kindle.
3. Rothstein. *The Color of Law,* n177, loc. 5856, Kindle.
4. "Investigation of the Ferguson Police Department," Department of Justice, March 4, 2015, p. 4.
5. "Investigation of the Ferguson Police Department," 2.
6. Otto Kerner, "Report of the National Advisory Commission on Civil Disorders," National Criminal Justice Reference Service, February 29, 1968, https://www.ncjrs.gov/pdffiles1/Digitization/8073NCJRS.pdf.
7. Cornel West, "Spiritual Blackout, Imperial Meltdown, Prophetic Fightback," speech, Askwith Forum, Harvard Graduate School of Education, October 4, 2017.
8. Julie Zauzmer, "Christians Are More than Twice as Likely to Blame a Person's Poverty on Lack of Effort," *Washington Post,* August 3, 2017, https://www.washingtonpost.com/news/acts-of -faith/wp/2017/08/03/christians-are-more-than-twice-as-likely-to -blame-a-persons-poverty-on-lack-of-effort/.
9. William A. Darity Jr. and A. Kirsten Mullen, *From Here to Equality: Reparations for Black Americans in the Twenty-First Century* (Chapel Hill: University of North Carolina Press, 2020), 30.
10. Ibram X. Kendi, *How to Be an Antiracist* (New York: One World, 2019), 18.
11. Kendi, *How to Be an Antiracist,* 18.
12. Deborah J. Vagins and Jesselyn McCurdy, "Cracks in the System: Twenty Years of the Unjust Federal Cocaine Law," ACLU,

October 2006, https://www.aclu.org/other/cracks-system-20-years
-unjust-federal-crack-cocaine-law.

13. Roger Taney, "The Dred Scott Decision," Library of Congress, 1857, https://www.loc.gov/item/17001543/.

14. Lori Rosza, "Voting Rights of Some Felons in Florida in Question after Appeals Court Ruling," *Washington Post*, July 8, 2020, https://www.washingtonpost.com/politics/voting-rights-of-some-felons-in-florida-in-question-after-appeals-court-ruling/2020/07/08/ad567af4-c116-11ea-9fdd-b7ac6b051dc8_story.html.

15. Ben Nadler, "Georgia Republican Candidate for Governor Puts 53,000 Voter Registrations on Hold," *USA Today*, October 11, 2018, https://www.usatoday.com/story/news/politics/elections/2018/10/11/georgia-republican-candidate-brian-kemp-puts-53-000-voter-registrations-hold/1608507002/.

16. Mark Niesse and Nick Thieme, "Precinct Closures Harm Voter Turnout in Georgia, AJC Analysis Finds," *Atlanta Journal-Constitution*, December 13, 2019, https://www.ajc.com/news/state—regional-govt—politics/precinct-closures-harm-voter-turnout-georgia-ajc-analysis-finds/11sVcLyQCHuQRC8qtZ6lYP/.

17. John Roberts, "Shelby County, Alabama v. Holder, Attorney General, et al.," Supreme Court of the United States, 679 F. 3d 848, reversed (June 25, 2013), p. 3.

18. Roberts, "Shelby County," 33.

19. Matt Vasilogambros, "Polling Places Remain a Target Ahead of November Elections," Pew: Stateline, September 4, 2018, https://www.pewtrusts.org/en/research-and-analysis/blogs/stateline/2018/09/04/polling-places-remain-a-target-ahead-of-november-elections.

20. Kara Brandeisky, Hanqing Chen, and Mike Tigas, "Everything That's Happened Since Supreme Court Ruled on Voting Rights Act," *ProPublica*, November 4, 2014, https://www.propublica.org/article/voting-rights-by-state-map.

21. Justin Levitt, "A Comprehensive Investigation of Voter Impersonation Finds 31 Credible Incidents Out of One Billion Ballots Cast," *Washington Post*, August 6, 2014, https://www.washingtonpost.com/news/wonk/wp/2014/08/06/a-comprehensive-investigation-of-voter-impersonation-finds-31-credible-incidents-out-of-one-billion-ballots-cast/.

22. "United States Court of Appeals for the Fourth Circuit: No. 14–1468," *United States Court of Appeals for the Fourth Circuit:*

Opinions, 11. http://www.ca4.uscourts.gov/Opinions/Published /161468.P.pdf.

23. German Lopez, "Florida Votes to Restore Ex-Felon Voting Rights with Amendment 4," Vox, November 7, 2018, https://www.vox .com/policy-and-politics/2018/11/6/18052374/florida-amendment -4-felon-voting-rights-results.

24. Drew Desilver, "U.S. Trails Most Developed Countries in Voter Turnout," Pew Research Center, May 21, 2018, https://www.pew research.org/fact-tank/2018/05/21/u-s-voter-turnout-trails-most -developed-countries/.

25. "Your Border Crisis Questions, Answered, Part 2," World Relief, August 8, 2019, https://worldrelief.org/your-border-crisis -questions-answered-part-2/.

26. Laura Barrón-López and Alex Thompson, "Biden under Fire for Mass Deportations under Obama," *Politico*, July 12, 2019, https:// www.politico.com/story/2019/07/12/biden-immigration-2020 –1411691.

27. John D. Skrentny and Jane Lilly López, "Obama's Immigration Reform: The Triumph of Executive Action," *Indiana Journal of Law and Social Equity* 2, no. 1 (2013), https://www.repository.law. indiana.edu/ijlse/vol2/iss1/3.

28. John Gramlich, "How Border Apprehensions, ICE Arrests and Deportations Have Changed under Trump," Pew Research Center: Fact Tank, March 2, 2020, https://www.pewresearch.org/ fact-tank/2020/03/02/how-border-apprehensions-ice-arrests-and -deportations-have-changed-under-trump/.

29. "Your Border Questions, Answered, Part 2."

30. "DACA," Immigrant Legal Resource Center, https://www.ilrc.org /daca.

31. Elaine Godfrey, "What 'Abolish ICE' Actually Means," *The Atlantic*, July 11, 2018, https://www.theatlantic.com/politics/archive/2018/07 /what-abolish-ice-actually-means/564752/.

32. Visit https://justicecorps.org/.

33. Visit https://worldrelief.org/.

34. Brooke Singman, "McConnell Says Stimulus Checks Would Go to Most Americans, as Senators Eye Higher Amount," Fox News, March 19, 2020, https://www.foxnews.com/politics/mcconnell-says -stimulus-checks-would-go-to-most-americans-as-senators-eye -higher-amount.

35. Leon LeBrecque, "The CARES Act Has Passed: Here Are The Highlights," *Forbes*, March 29, 2020, https://www.forbes.com /sites/leonlabrecque/2020/03/29/the-cares-act-has-passed-here -are-the-highlights/#4035871a68cd.

36. William A. Darity Jr. and A. Kirsten Mullen, *From Here to Equality: Reparations for Black Americans in the Twenty-First Century* (Chapel Hill: University of North Carolina Press, 2020), 31.

37. Tanvi Misra, "It Could Take 2 Centuries For Racial Wealth Disparities to Dissipate," CityLab, August 9, 2016, https://www .citylab.com/life/2016/08/it-could-take-2-centuries-for-wealth -disparities-to-dissipate-between-whites-and-blacks/495092/.

38. Darity and Mullen, *From Here to Equality*, 2.

39. Darity and Mullen, *From Here to Equality*, 2.

40. Darity and Mullen, *From Here to Equality*, 4.

41. William Darity Jr. and A. Kirsten Mullen. "How Reparations for American Descendants of Slavery Could Narrow the Racial Wealth Divide," NBC: Think, June 20, 2019, https://www.nbc news.com/think/opinion/how-reparations-american-descendants -slavery-could-narrow-racial-wealth-divide-ncna1019691.

42. There is some debate about whether any African-descended people, including immigrants who arrived after the abolition of slavery, would be eligible for reparations. The African Descendants of Slavery (ADOS) movement advocates for a narrow interpretation of eligibility that would not include immigrants. The movement has been accused of fomenting xenophobic ideas, and William Darity Jr. has come under criticism for associating with them. See Wesley Lowery, "Which Black Americans Should Get Reparations?," *Washington Post*, September 18, 2019, https://www.washingtonpost.com/national /which-americans-should-get-reparations/2019/09/18/271cf744 -cab1–11e9-a4f3-c081a126de70_story.html.

43. Darity and Mullen, *From Here to Equality*, 258.

44. William A. Darity Jr., "Reparations," *Encyclopedia of African-American Culture and History*, ed. Colin A. Palmer, 2nd ed., vol. 5 (Detroit: Macmillan Reference, 2006), 1924–28.

45. "H.R.40—Commission to Study and Develop Reparation Proposals for African-Americans Act," Congress.gov, https://www .congress.gov/bill/116th-congress/house-bill/40.

46. Personal email correspondence with the pastor, March 25, 2020.

47. Michael Lomax, "Why HBCUs Still Matter," United Negro
    College Fund, https://uncf.org/the-latest/why-hbcus-still-matter.
48. Jesse J. Smith, "'Reparations Pricing': Kingston Event Asks
    Whites to Pay; Offers Free Admission for People of Color,"
    Hudson Valley One, September 21, 2018, https://hudsonvalleyone
    .com/2018/09/21/reparations-pricing-kingston-event-asks-whites
    -to-pay-offers-free-admission-for-people-of-color/.
49. "Ahmaud Arbery Murder Investigation," Georgia Bureau of
    Investigations, https://gbi.georgia.gov/press-releases/2020–05–21
    /ahmaud-arbery-murder-investigation.
50. Malcolm X, TV interview, March 1964, https://www.youtube.com
    /watch?v=XiSiHRNQlQo.
51. L. G. Shivers, "A History of the Mississippi Penitentiary," as quoted
    in David Oshinsky, *Worse Than Slavery: Parchman Farm and the
    Ordeal of Jim Crow Justice* (New York: Simon & Schuster, 1996), 3.
52. Bryan Stevenson, *Just Mercy: A Story of Justice and Redemption*
    (New York: Spiegel & Grau, 2014), 290.
53. Ashley Nellis, "The Color of Justice: Racial and Ethnic Disparity
    in State Prisons," The Sentencing Project, June 14, 2016.
54. Nellis, "The Color of Justice."
55. "14 and 21-Year Old Negroes Executed in Electric Chair," *The
    Greenville News*, June 17, 1944.
56. Bill Chappell. "S.C. Judge Says 1944 Execution Of 14-Year-Old
    Boy Was Wrong" *The Two-Way*, NPR, December 17, 2014, https://
    www.npr.org/sections/thetwo-way/2014/12/17/371534533/s-c-judge
    -says-boy-14-shouldn-t-have-been-executed.
57. "Fact Sheet," Death Penalty Information Center, https://files
    .deathpenaltyinfo.org/documents/pdf/FactSheet.f1585003454.pdf.
58. "NAACP Death Penalty Fact Sheet," NAACP, November 17, 2017,
    https://www.naacp.org/latest/naacp-death-penalty-fact-sheet/#_edn6.
59. "A Clear Scientific Consensus that the Death Penalty Does Not
    Deter," Amnesty International, https://www.amnestyusa.org/a
    -clear-scientific-consensus-that-the-death-penalty-does-not
    -deter/; "Death Penalty," Equal Justice Initiative, https://eji.org
    /issues/death-penalty/.
60. "The Case Against the Death Penalty," ACLU, https://www.aclu
    .org/other/case-against-death-penalty.
61. Jennifer Gonnerman, "Before the Law," *New Yorker*, September 29,
    2014, https://www.newyorker.com/magazine/2014/10/06/before-the-law.

62. Gonnerman, "Before the Law."

63. Elaine Low, "'Let's Keep Fighting': 'Just Mercy's' Bryan Stevenson Urges Advocacy at NAACP Image Awards," *Variety*, February 22, 2020, https://variety.com/2020/tv/news/naacp -image-awards-bryan-stevenson-just-mercy-1203511883/.

64. "The Black Panther Party's Ten-Point Program," hosted by the UC Press Blog, University of California Press, February 7, 2020, https://www.ucpress.edu/blog/25139/the-black-panther-partys-ten -point-program/. Capitalization original.

65. Mariam Kaba. "Yes, We Mean Literally Abolish the Police," *New York Times*, June 12, 2020, https://www.nytimes.com/2020/06/12 /opinion/sunday/floyd-abolish-defund-police.html.

66. Angela Davis. "Angela Davis on Abolition, Calls to Defund Police, Toppled Racist Statues & Voting in 2020 Election," Democracy Now, July 3, 2020, https://www.democracynow.org/2020/7/3 /angela_davis_on_abolition_calls_to.

67. Some activists note, for instance, that without strict rules and guidance, police body cameras can be used as another form of state surveillance. See "Police Body Cameras," ACLU, https://www.aclu.org/issues/privacy-technology/surveillance -technologies/police-body-cameras.

68. Sarah Mervosh, "How Much Wealthier Are White School Districts Than Nonwhite Ones? $23 Billion, Report Says," *New York Times*, February 27, 2019, https://www.nytimes.com/2019 /02/27/education/school-districts-funding-white-minorities.html.

69. Tawnelle D. Hobbs, "In Mississippi, an Unlikely Model for School Desegregation," *Wall Street Journal*, November 22, 2019, https:// www.wsj.com/articles/in-mississippi-an-unlikely-model-for-school -desegregation-11574424004.

70. Elise C. Boddie and Dennis D. Parker, "Linda Brown and the Unfinished Work of School Integration," *New York Times*, March 30, 2018, https://www.nytimes.com/2018/03/30/opinion/linda -brown-school-integration.html.

Chapter 10: How to Orient Your Life to Racial Justice

1. John M. Gottman and Nan Silver, *The Seven Principles for Making Marriage Work: A Practical Guide from the Country's Foremost Relationship Expert*, 2nd ed. (New York: Harmony, 2015), 34.

2. Gottman and Silver, *The Seven Principles for Making Marriage Work*, 34.

3. Ellie Lisitsa, "The Four Horsemen: Contempt," *The Gottman Relationship Blog*, May 13, 2013, https://www.gottman.com/blog /the-four-horsemen-contempt/.

4. Stuart Walton, "The World of G. K. Chesterton, and What's Wrong with It," *Guardian*, January 8, 2010, https://www.theguardian.com /books/booksblog/2010/jan/08/gk-chesterton-world-whats-wrong.

5. Andy Kiersz, "Here's How Much the Average Wall Street Banker Makes at Each Stage of Their Career," *Business Insider*, July 13, 2018, https://www.businessinsider.com/wall-street-salary-how -much-bankers-make-2018–7.

6. "Graham Smith Named CCCU Young Alumni Award Winner," Council of Christian Colleges and Universities: News and Publications, November 22, 2019, https://www.cccu.org/news -updates/graham-smith-named-cccu-young-alumni-award -winner/.

7. Jason "Propaganda" Petty, "Precious Puritans," featuring Kevin 'K.O.' Olusola, track 7 on *Excellent*, Humble Beast, 2012.

8. Petty, "Precious Puritans."

9. Chris Joyner, "Georgia Mayor under Fire for Alleged Remarks about Black Job Candidate," *Atlanta Journal-Constitution*, May 6, 2019, https://www.ajc.com/news/local-govt—politics/georgia -mayor-under-fire-for-alleged-remarks-about-black-job-candidate /Qr403ZLnF5VuB8CzpngLjP/?fbclid=IwAR0f8pcGjO7Ehg33Xl 9Qz-FKnjfrsa8Cb-BBO5fvYu27–8d36H1MHPA4UBE.

10. Michael Brice-Saddler, "A Mayor Reportedly Said Her City Isn't Ready for a Black Leader. A Council Member Went Further," *Washington Post*, May 8, 2019, https://www.washingtonpost.com /politics/2019/05/08/mayor-reportedly-said-her-city-isnt-ready -black-leader-council-member-went-further/.

11. Ryan Wilson, "Donald Trump: NFL Should Have Suspended Colin Kaepernick for Kneeling," CBS Sports, October 12, 2017, https://www.cbssports.com/nfl/news/donald-trump-nfl-should -have-suspended-colin-kaepernick-for-kneeling/.

12. "Our Mission," Know Your Rights Camp, https://www.knowyour rightscamp.com/.

13. Michael Martin, "The Veteran and NFL Player Who Advised Kaepernick to Take a Knee," *All Things Considered*, NPR,

September 9, 2018, https://www.npr.org/2018/09/09/646115651/the
-veteran-and-nfl-player-who-advised-kaepernick-to-take-a-knee.

14. Steven J. Gaither. "Five-Star Makur Maker Officially Commits
to Howard University," HBCU Gameday, July 3, 2020, https://
hbcugameday.com/2020/07/03/five-star-makur-maker-commits-to
-howard-university/#:~:text=Makur%20Maker%2C%20a%20five
%2Dstar,to%20dream%20%E2%80%9Cwhat%20if%E2%80%9D.

15. Brian Morton, "Falser Words Were Never Spoken," *New York
Times*, August 29, 2011, https://www.nytimes.com/2011/08/30
/opinion/falser-words-were-never-spoken.html.

16. Aleksandra Sandstrom, "5 Facts about the Religious Makeup of
the 116th Congress," Pew Research Center: Fact Tank, January
3, 2019, https://www.pewresearch.org/fact-tank/2019/01/03/5
-facts-about-the-religious-makeup-of-the-116th-congress/.

17. Nikole Hannah-Jones, "Choosing a School for My Daughter in
a Segregated City," *New York Times*, June 9, 2016, https://www
.nytimes.com/2016/06/12/magazine/choosing-a-school-for-my
-daughter-in-a-segregated-city.html.

18. Hannah-Jones, "Choosing a School for My Daughter in a
Segregated City."

Conclusion

1. Fannie Lou Hamer, *The Speeches of Fannie Lou Hamer: To Tell
It Like It Is*, ed. Maegan Parker Brooks and Davis W. Houck
(Jackson: University Press of Mississippi, 2011), 6.

2. Kay Mills, *This Little Light of Mine: The Life of Fannie Lou
Hamer* (Lexington: University Press of Kentucky, 2007), 308.

3. Mills, *This Little Light of Mine*, 308.

4. John Dittmer. *Local People: The Struggle for Civil Rights in
Mississippi* (Urbana: University of Illinois Press, 1994), 433.

5. Hamer, *Speeches*, 4.